When the State Knocks
A Parent's Guide to CPS (Child Protective Services)

I0202585

Michael H. Agranoff

Table of Contents

Copyright

WHEN THE STATE KNOCKS:

A Parent's Guide to CPS (Child Protective Services)

By Atty. Michael H. Agranoff

Ellington, CT, USA

CHAPTER 1: INTRODUCTION TO CPS

Every State in the United States has a child protective service, or CPS. The major purpose of CPS is to protect children from abuse or neglect, whether by parents, guardians, or other persons.

CPS agencies are known by different acronyms, such as DCF, DCYS, DCYF, DHS, OCFS, and others. New York City even has its own CPS, known as ACS (Administration for Children's Services). How this came to be, and what it means, we shall discover.

In ancient Rome, parents had life and death power over their children. Today we are more enlightened. But not everyone knows how easy it is today for the State to interfere in your family life. It can seize your children temporarily. In some cases it can end your parental rights altogether.

CPS and the courts can interfere in your family life in several ways, including:

1. Investigating your family and suggesting rules for you to follow, under their supervision.

2. Placing you on the Child Abuse Registry. This prevents you from getting employment in many fields.

3. Hauling you into Juvenile Court, and asking the Judge to place you under orders known as "protective supervision", or PS. If you do not follow these rules, your kids may be removed. Sometimes they may be removed even if you do. Note: In New York and some other states, Juvenile Court is referred to as Family Court.

4. Asking the Judge to remove your children temporarily (or longer) and placing them with other relatives or in foster homes. If the kids are unlucky or too obstinate, they may be placed in group homes.

5. Asking the Judge to terminate your parental rights, known as TPR. TPR is the ultimate sanction, a parental death sentence. It permanently severs the legal bond of parent and child.

CPS has a serious and important job, and there are many good or excellent CPS social workers. But like all government agencies, CPS often overreaches. The goals of this essay are:

To alert parents to the present dangers of CPS;

To advise parents how to protect themselves and their kids;

To warn Americans of future CPS encroachments.

I will discuss several CPS cases, all from my own 31 years of experience as a CPS defense lawyer. These occurred in Connecticut but could have happened anywhere. All persons are identified by pseudonyms, except where full names are used. All are real individuals; no conglomerates.

And I swear on my grandkids, no facts are made up or exaggerated. There is no need.

All parents need to be on guard. Your social standing or community reputation makes no difference.

Finally, I will discuss CPS dangers that are not here yet but are on the horizon, such as the licensing of parents. We need to ensure that they do not happen.

.

On occasion I have inserted some humorous items. I trust that no one will be offended. Movies may show life as either a comedy or a drama, but in truth it is both. Please, whatever you do, never lose your ability to see how silly some things are.

IMPORTANT DISCLAIMER: This essay does NOT constitute specific legal advice. It is not intended as a substitute for contacting a qualified CPS defense lawyer. Receipt of this information does NOT create or constitute an attorney-client relationship.

CHAPTER 2: IT'S MY TEDDY BEAR

When the entire world tells you that you're wrong, it's a good bet that you are. But a good bet is not necessarily a sure thing.

I got a call from Alice and Peter. CPS had taken their kids and wanted TPR.

They were on their third lawyer. In many cases, parents cannot afford a CPS lawyer, so the State gives them a State-paid lawyer; whose quality, shall we say, varies greatly. Alice and Peter had a privately paid lawyer and expected good results. However, their lawyer did nothing but agree with CPS. They were desperate.

I took the case. Of course, clients seldom tell you everything. Here is what I found upon reviewing the huge court file:

1. Alice had a long-standing drinking problem. She minimized it and refused to cooperate with treatment.

2. Peter was violent towards Alice. The kids (Hank, age 10 and Sharon, age 14) had witnessed that.

3. Both parents refused to properly supervise the kids. Hank was traumatized. Sharon was parentified (having to function as an adult before she was ready to do so). Both kids were afraid of their parents.

4. The kids had been removed before, then returned when the family got its act together. Then the parents relapsed, and the kids were taken again.

5. The kids were placed with Alice's mother, whom Alice positively hated. Alice said that her mother had been abusive to her as a child. The mother said that Alice was just a difficult child. She said/she said in the extreme.

6. The parents had not had 3 lawyers, as they told me. They had 5 prior lawyers. I was now 6th on the roster. As every law office practice manual will tell you, this is a sure-fire red flag to avoid the case.

7. Sharon had been allowed to testify against her parents at a prior hearing and really gave them what-for. This was unusual. Kids are generally not allowed to testify at CPS hearings but must do so through their lawyer. (The State automatically gives the kids a lawyer in CPS

matters. They cannot hire their own, through their parents or others. That would be a conflict of interest).

8. Alice was an unrelenting arguer, another red flag. No matter what services were offered to her, she argued with the providers, driving them to despair. No one would work with her any longer. Peter, a low-key man, could not control her.

And that was just from the court file. At a pretrial hearing (which means that everyone is present except the trial Judge), I got worse of an earful:

1. According to the CPS lawyer, TPR was a foregone conclusion.

2. The kids had separate lawyers. Sharon's lawyer hated Alice with a passion and had little use for Peter. She was firm that TPR had to happen.

3. Hank had a lawyer, but he almost never saw Hank (state pay is low). That lawyer just kept saying that things were fine.

4. The kids had the same therapist, whom we will call Ms. Smoothie. She insisted that both kids had told her that they wanted TPR from both parents.

So that's what I walked into.

The latest document in the case file was a 22-page single-spaced paper called the "CPS Social Study." That is a mandatory document that requires CPS to present its findings and support its recommendations. I read the study word-for-word, which the prior lawyers had apparently not done. There were two possible smoking guns.

On pages 4-5 of the study were a few paragraphs stating that Alice was meeting with a forensic clinical psychologist, whom we will call Dr. Jung. Dr. Jung said that he had made great progress in helping Alice deal with her emotional problems. Jung had also worked with Peter and believed that family reunification was possible. What is strange is that Dr. Jung's comments were not mentioned in the study's final summary or case recommendations.

On pages 20-21 of the study was Ms. Smoothie's statement, already mentioned, that she had discussed TPR with the kids and both favored it. This was incredible, since TPR is a so-called "adult issue." Therapists and guardians are generally forbidden to discuss adult issues with kids in CPS matters. They are supposed to focus on treatment and therapy instead. Ms.

6

Smoothie, not a lawyer, had allegedly discussed a complicated legal matter with a 10-year-old boy. I was inclined to not believe her statement.

It should be noted that CPS itself selects the therapists. It is a competitive field. It is surely not impossible that contracted therapists would tell their payor what they wanted to hear.

Armed with these two tidbits, I fought the matter in court. I insisted that Hank not be brainwashed in therapy. I got Dr. Jung's comments, and some additional written comments, to the attention of the Court and to the other lawyers and therapists. CPS then lied and said that they had seen Dr. Jung's original statement and had tried to contact him but were unable to do so. That is simply not even possible with a licensed and available professional. I insisted that Hank's lawyer actually visit him and speak to him privately.

I filed a motion for more visitation between the kids and the parents, which CPS objected to.

ASIDE. A motion is nothing more than a request for a court order during the pendency of the case, or sometimes after it is over (such as in a divorce post-judgment motion for more child support). It simply asks for a ruling by the Judge.

A hearing was scheduled. When CPS saw Dr. Jung in the hallway, ready to testify, they dropped their opposition without having the hearing! The visitation was small, but it was a start. The inference is that CPS knew it had no credible reason to oppose visitation.

I also got CPS to stop harassing Alice and Peter. If they wanted anything, they had to go through me. Lay persons must understand that while this is standard in criminal and civil matters, it is customary in CPS matters for social workers to contact parents directly. CPS knows that the parents' lawyers often don't want to be bothered.

But best of all, I got CPS to admit that their two major arguments were no longer true: Alice had been substance-free for three years (we produced the test results, which incredibly CPS claimed not to have seen!); and the couple had had no incidents of domestic violence in 3-1/2 years (we produced police records and testimony).

CPS then assigned a new social worker, as they often do, and this one was patient and reasonable. Then CPS agreed to drop its plans for TPR. Sharon would stay with her grandmother for now, and Hank would be gradually reunified with his parents. This meant: more day visits; then overnights visits; and eventual return.

Meanwhile, Alice had gotten pregnant. She was terrified that CPS would take the new baby. Problems never end. However, I made sure through some tough letters that this did not happen.

So far, so good; but all good things must come to an end.

Sharon's lawyer, whom you recall hated Alice, threatened to file a TPR for Sharon on her own if CPS did not do so. The law allowed the lawyer to do this.

It seemed like an idle threat, but the lawyer had her own smoking gun. It seems that Sharon had asked Alice to return a teddy bear that was hers as a child. Alice, true to form, stubbornly refused to do so. Sharon's lawyer then filed a court motion to order her to do so.

ASIDE. In the old days of the English common law, the motions that a lawyer could file were strictly limited to accepted forms. Nowadays, virtually any motion can be filed. A friend once told me that he was going to file a motion to declare that opposing counsel was an idiot. Weird motions are not uncommon in emotional matters; but a motion to return a teddy bear may have been a first.

Alice, characteristically, refused to return the teddy bear, claiming that it was "lost." In reality, she did not want to appear to "give in." So the lawyer wanted Alice's parental rights to Sharon terminated over a stuffed toy. The lawyer's pressure caused CPS to cave in and file for TPR regarding Sharon only, not Hank.

We contested the TPR and had a good case. Several experts testified that TPR was not a good idea, especially as reunification for Hank was progressing, and siblings should not be separated. Alice's mother herself said that she would be happy with only a simple transfer of guardianship. That means she would keep custody of Sharon, but not formally end Alice's parental rights. Amazingly, even Ms. Smoothie was equivocal on the stand. But once again, Sharon herself was allowed to testify, and strongly asked for TPR.

The Judge granted TPR. I am convinced he did it just to get rid of the whole mess. As for Sharon, when she gets older and has children of her own, she may look at things differently. Ain't it the truth.

Finally, some 17-1/2 months after I was hired on this impossible case with all enemies and no allies, Hank was returned to his parents. I am told that he and his baby brother get along well. And Grandma does allow him to see Sharon.

Alice and Peter are hardly saints, but kids belong with their parents unless that is impossible or impracticable. Had TPR happened for Hank, his life might have been ruined. That is something that CPS defense lawyers should take more seriously.

Why had I succeeded (in part) when five previous lawyers had failed?

It certainly isn't because I'm brilliant, and I'm not just saying that out of modesty. My LSAT (Law School Admissions Test) scores were average. My law school grades were good (magna cum laude), but that was because I had the benefit of years of business experience and was organized. I could not, and still cannot, understand the opinions of Justice Rehnquist. I passed the Connecticut Bar on my first try, but the scores were nothing to write home about. Hardly Clarence Darrow.

The main reason is that I refused to accept what was said and written until I had personally verified it. Also, I had the old-fashioned idea that families were the core of society.

If I hadn't suspected that CPS was wrong and worked to prove it, Hank would have been traumatized for life. Sometimes you have to speak up. As to the other lawyers who refused to work the case seriously: where was your sense of responsibility?

CHAPTER 3: TO PROTECT THE GUILTY

Roberta and Alex had 3 kids, boys of 16 (Jeremy) and 11 (Harry) and a girl of 9 (Carrie). Alex was a pleasant man with a very good job, and Roberta was an excellent homemaker. It seemed like the ideal middle-class family. But as we see in TV dramas, there was a secret: Jeremy had severe emotional problems.

One day Jeremy touched Carrie improperly. Carrie got scared and told a teacher, who told the police. Then Carrie changed her story to say that her father Alex had touched her. The police threatened to arrest Alex.

Roberta was beside herself. She knew her husband would not do this, and she knew how kids were influenced by what they heard at school. Roberta made a lot of noise and did everything other than call a lawyer. [One of my standard web site sayings was that as soon as you are threatened by CPS or police, you should call a lawyer. You do not fool around on the internet or talk to friends or argue with people. I often felt like a modern-day Cassandra]. The upshot was that Roberta herself was threatened with arrest for obstruction of justice!

Now Alex finally got one of the top criminal lawyers in the State, but it was too late. If Alex went to trial and was found guilty, he would face a long prison term, Roberta would likely be arrested, and all 3 kids taken away. So Alex bit the bullet and plead guilty to something he did not do. He got a reduced sentence and a promise that Roberta would not be prosecuted. He was eventually released. No criminal charges were pressed against Roberta, and Jeremy began receiving treatment.

CPS had of course been called in the interim. As soon as Alex went to jail, CPS removed Carrie from the home. Harry was allowed to stay, provided that Jeremy moved out.

At that point, Roberta composed herself and called a lawyer. We shall call her Atty. Stentor (you can look that up, the loudmouth from the Iliad.) Atty. Stentor is a formidable woman who yells and screams and badgers and belittles opposing counsel to their faces. She threatens and makes innumerable phone calls and sends tons of e-mails. She is, to be polite, a gigantic pain in the neck.

The problem is that all of Atty. Stentor's bluff and bluster accomplished nothing; mere smoke and mirrors. After 3-1/2 years, Carrie was no closer to coming home, Roberta had paid her $25,000.00 and just received a bill for another $35,000.00 due. 60 Grand for nothing.

At that point Roberta knew that she had been had, and somehow found me.

I told her to bring all of her paperwork to the office, in chronological order. I did not B.S. her and spend hours listening to her vent, which would have been a colossal waste of time. Fortunately, Roberta kept good records, including all of her correspondence with Atty. Stentor. Among my findings in reviewing the file:

1. Atty. Stentor had had numerous e-mail conferences with various service providers (therapists and the like), asking them what they thought. One thing you learn in law or any other business is that when you have a problem, you never ask other people what they think you should do without first telling them what you think you need to do. They are not going to do your work for you. They will recognize that you are uncomfortable with the case and are just fishing.

2. Carrie's therapist said that the reunification process should begin. In fact, the CPS permanency plan itself (a requirement mandated by federal law) called for reunification.

3. Roberta had an individual therapist whom she saw regularly. She attended meetings at Carrie's school. She interacted well with Carrie's foster parents.

4. Atty. Stentor never filed a motion for reunification (technically, a motion to revoke the commitment). She had none of the two facts above in her notes. Also absent was Atty. Stentor's interaction with the social worker, who was openly hostile to Roberta.

5. Carrie had a court-appointed lawyer. She had never once seen Carrie, attended a school meeting, or interviewed Roberta or the foster parents! For those who have trouble believing this, you ain't seen nuthin' yet. CPS defense - if nothing else - is a laugh a minute. Atty. Stentor filed no motion to compel visits with their client.

It became clear that the basis of CPS's hostility was their belief that Roberta had "chosen" the father over the child. In actual fact, she had chosen her oldest child over the father. There was evidence that some CPS workers already suspected that.

I took over the case and filed the paperwork to replace Atty. Stentor.

I began the case by writing to CPS and asking exactly what Roberta was doing that she should not be doing, or was not doing what she should be doing, as an obstacle to reunification. Apparently knowing that the jig was up, they simply stonewalled me; an old bureaucratic trick.

I wrote to the social work supervisor; also no luck. I then wrote to the CPS Ombudsman, and that worked. I got some answers, not totally satisfactory.

I then spoke to Roberta's CPS-provided psychologist. The psychologist was very cooperative and stated clearly that there should be overnight visits and a definite reunification plan put in place right away. However, she was reluctant to put that in writing. She was apparently afraid to tell her CPS benefactors what they didn't want to hear.

Undaunted, I drafted a letter for the psychologist, based on her own statements, and sent a copy to CPS and to Carrie's lawyers. That got her to move: she wrote her own letter two weeks later, and that became our smoking gun.

I also obtained statements from Carrie's school and got their treatment plan, which was very favorable. I got statements from the foster parents and from Carrie's individual therapist. I pressured Carrie's lawyer to actually (God save the mark!) visit Carrie. To counter her expected reluctance and alibis, I provided the address, phone number and e-mail of the foster parents. There was no way out (apologies to Kevin Costner), and she finally saw the kid.

Then I filed a motion to revoke the commitment. This meant that CPS would return Carrie to Roberta with "specific steps." These are court-ordered restrictions in place, and services to be offered, supervised by CPS. Knowing that CPS would resist every way it could, I drafted the motion to include every single case detail, hoping that would make CPS give in.

And give in they did. Apparently when the CPS lawyer saw my motion, he hit the roof, called CPS, and "advised" them to cooperate. The motion was granted without opposition. Three months later, Carrie was returned under PS for 6 months, meaning that if all went well, CPS would be totally out of the picture.

But CPS hates to lose. The social worker was just as angry at Roberta as ever. After Carrie was returned under PS, she told Roberta that CPS had set her up in a class for "sexual abuse non-offenders" at a local clinic, so that Roberta would "better understand the issues"; but that Roberta had failed to attend. She threatened to file a motion to reinstate the commitment (remove the child again). The social worker did not have the decency to tell me this, only to harass Roberta. But of course Roberta told me.

I called the clinic and verified that the class had not yet started, due to lack of enrollment; but they would tell me when it opened.

I told the social worker, who again ignored me. Same result with the supervisor. I wrote again to the CPS Ombudsman, who by now must have been wondering what was going on in this case. Finally, CPS relented, and PS ended as scheduled.

Carrie is now at home. She continued to see her therapist but is barred from seeing her father until she is 18 (which is the case by now). By all accounts, she is doing well. I am told that the older brother underwent serious treatment. I hope so.

And whose fault was this near massacre? No one's, of course. It's just the system. No one takes responsibility in a bureaucracy. No one is above lack of integrity, or outright lying, to make a point.

On a happy note, I took Atty. Stentor's bill for $35,000.00 and wrote to her. I asked her to explain the reasonableness of a bill totaling $60,000.00 for doing nothing for 3 years. There was no reply. So, I lost a friend, but it wasn't the first time. At least a few score hours of real work and attention to detail overcame 3 years of inaction.

If Roberta had simply told CPS what they wanted to hear (Alex was a child molester), the couple would have split forever, a lie perpetrated, and Jeremy would probably have gotten no help. If I had not been proactive with CPS, their vindictive actions would have been rewarded.

CHAPTER 4: SPARE THE ROD AND SPOIL THE CHILD

I always said that if you had any dealings with CPS, even seemingly friendly ones, the first thing you should do is to call a CPS defense lawyer. Was this a sneaky attempt to drum up business? Was this being paranoid? After all, you do not hire a liquor lawyer every time you walk into a bar.

Two little girls, one age 2, one only 4 months, were being taken from their parents. The parents would be TPR'd. No one disputed this. The parents had severe drug and mental health problems and were unfit to raise children by anyone's standards.

The paternal grandmother was frantic at the thought of foster care and possible adoption of her granddaughters by strangers. She herself was not able to care for them, but she knew that her brother and his wife were solid people, loved children, and had a wonderful home. They were perfect as placement resources, and eventual adoptive parents.

The brother's name was Bernard. He had an adult son from a prior marriage and had recently married Elizabeth. They were moderately educated, in their 50's, of high moral character, and known to family and friends as superb people. Elizabeth herself had never had children but frequently babysat for friends and relatives. In earlier years, she had practically raised a nephew whose parents had had problems.

Bernard and Elizabeth agreed to take in the girls. It didn't take long for the CPS social worker to investigate them and their house and place the girls with them. It was "understood" that when TPR went through, Bernard and Elizabeth would be the #1 favorites for adoption. An excellent job by CPS, and the system was working.

All was going well. Perhaps too well. At Christmas time, Elizabeth had a thought. It was one that she would regret for the rest of her life.

Elizabeth told Bernard that since things were going very well, it might be nice if they could adopt a boy about the age as the older girl. Bernard agreed, and they called CPS.

The CPS social worker told them that she did not have a boy, but she did have a girl just a few years older. She was healthy, friendly, and doing well in school. Unfortunately, it could only be a temporary placement. Bernard and Elizabeth were disappointed, but not wishing to appear ungrateful for the opportunity, agreed to take in the kid.

Sadly, the new girl turned out to be the dreaded "foster child from Hell." She had been physically and sexually abused and was aggressive, disrespectful, mean, and a chronic liar. She was extremely jealous of any attention paid to other children. She was in therapy, but no one had been able to help her. She had disrupted 5 placements in 2 years. This means that the foster parents had given up and called CPS to take her away.

The girl clearly needed a therapeutic foster home, with adults specially trained to handle severe problem cases; or else needed to be institutionalized. But the social worker had told Bernard and Elizabeth none of this. She had obviously been unsuccessful in placing the girl. She must have thought that she had died and gone to Heaven when the couple called her: another problem to be cleared out of her in-box. So what if it was a "white" lie. The greater good, you know.

Over the months, Bernard and Elizabeth told several CPS social workers that the girl needed to be in a home where she was the only child. They got a lot of sympathy but nothing else. One worker did ask them if they wanted the child removed. Here Bernard and Elizabeth made another grave but innocent mistake: not wanting to appear as "quitters", they said No. They would regret that also.

Things continued to go badly, and Elizabeth spanked the girl a few times. It is uncontroverted that these were light spankings. However, the girl told her therapist, who told CPS, and an investigation began.

There is considerable debate on whether corporal punishment of children is productive or even humane. I will not get into that, although I note that a potsch in tuchas, as we say in Yiddish, is sometimes necessary. At present, Connecticut state law considers reasonable parental and custodial discipline to not be assault.

However, CPS is solidly against corporal punishment of children for any reason. It forbids corporal punishment of kids in foster care.

Elizabeth signed several documents, one of which stated this. But obviously she forgot it.

When the investigation began, CPS did not tell the couple that they could have a lawyer present. They were nervous and made comments that they later regretted. As a result, CPS pulled not only the Brat From Hell, but the two great-nieces as well. Rubbing salt on the wound, CPS recommended both Bernard and Elizabeth for placement on the Child Abuse Registry.

Yes, I know. You don't believe it. But it's true.

At this point, the couple called me. We began by appealing the Registry placements. These appeals are done administratively at a CPS office and heard by a CPS Hearing Officer who is a lawyer. If you lose, you can appeal to the Superior Court.

Some bright CPS in-house lawyer must have read the file and had Bernard removed from the Registry before the hearing even began! At the hearing, for Elizabeth only, I got testimony from friends and relatives and the girls' court-appointed lawyer; none of whom CPS had contacted in its "investigation." As a result, the Registry placement for Elizabeth was also reversed.

Meantime, the Juvenile Court was now ready to proceed on the CPS petitions for TPR regarding the two girls. The social workers, angry as always that they lost their Registry placements, refused to consider Bernard and Elizabeth as placement resources and adoptive parents. The girls remained with strangers.

The TPR hearing of the parents was of course in Juvenile Court. Such hearings are closed to the public, so I immediately filed a motion for intervention in the case. This means that we could participate in the otherwise closed CPS hearing. We could argue our case for return of the girls. Fortunately, the competent lawyer for the girls, who had spoken to the older girl, understood her wishes. She had also spoken to Bernard and Elizabeth and really understood the case. She went to bat for us.

But incredibly, the Judge denied our motion to intervene. The technical reason was that our intervention would unduly delay the proceedings. The real reason was that CPS had already found a suitable adoptive couple, and the Judge wanted to get the matter over with. [When a kid is TPR'd, CPS decides on the adoptive parents, and the Judge rubber-stamps it as a formality].

By a quirk in Connecticut law, denial of a motion to intervene in Juvenile Court is not appealable. So we were out for good.

Most Judges are the salt of the Earth, and I am not saying that this Judge was wrong – from his viewpoint. But what about the viewpoint of the girls, who wanted to be with their great-uncle and his wife? What about the viewpoint of Bernard and Elizabeth, who were great people and had been virtually promised adoption and believed they had no need for lawyers?

Call it just their tough luck. But believe it or not, we weren't done yet.

By now, Bernard and Elizabeth were out of money, so I did the rest of the case pro bono (for free). I really felt for these kindly and thoroughly decent folks.

I pleaded with CPS to allow visitation between Bernard and Elizabeth and the girls, even if supervised, before the adoption was finalized. CPS refused. I filed for a CPS Administrative Hearing to order visitation. The Hearing Officer ruled that in view of the TPR, he had no authority to order visitation. But he strongly recommended under the circumstances that CPS do so. There is no doubt in my mind that the Hearing Officer knew that CPS had wronged this couple.

After weeks of wrangling, CPS issued its final refusal. No visitation: not in the girls "best interests." We were finished, with no recourse.

The last e-mail I received from Bernard and Elizabeth said in part "We would like to thank you for trying your best. We hate [CPS] for what they did to us and those two precious babies. They were able to physically take them away from us, but they can never take the memories and love we will always have for them. It's a terrible, terrible thing that they have the power to do this to people. Again, many thanks for everything you did."

I can't say that it made me feel any better. While I've seen worse CPS cases, I've never seen one so cruel.

Don't bother writing to CPS for their side. "It's confidential."

One thing that emerges from this case is how willing people are to believe others just because they have a badge of authority. When President Reagan said, "Trust but verify," he was perhaps more correct than he realized.

So look at the result: two innocent little girls were taken away from loving family members for the flimsiest of reasons, caused initially by a bald-faced social worker lie, and abetted by their own naivete.

Integrity? When you consider how many people get away with murder, this punishment for Bernard and Elizabeth is enough to make you sick.

Responsibility? Rush to judgment to get rid of a case. As Pope wrote:

The hungry judges soon the sentence sign,
And wretches hang, that jurymen may dine.

So we are clear: most Judges are excellent. Some take no nonsense from CPS. But there's always the luck of the draw.

CHAPTER 5: WHERE THERE'S SMOKE, YOU MAY BE ON FIRE

Suppose you opened the newspaper to the following headline:
CPS HITS RURAL COUPLE WITH 12 CHARGES;
HUSBAND AND WIFE EACH ACCUSED OF BOTH MEDICAL NEGLECT AND PHYSICAL NEGLECT OF EACH OF THEIR 3 BOYS;
COUPLE INDIFFERENT TO KIDS' POTENTIAL BLINDNESS AND ROTTING TEETH;
COUPLE ALSO ARGUMENTATIVE AND UN-COOPERATIVE WITH CPS.

Your reaction? Of course, you wouldn't actually see this headline unless the couple were arrested, since CPS matters are confidential. But what would you think if you did? Yes, I know; there must be some truth to it. CPS social workers are dedicated and trained, and many have Masters' degrees. Most likely, you would be angry that in our civilized country, this could happen to innocent kids. I wouldn't blame you. Where there's smoke, there's fire.

Now you read the full article and see some gory details: all 3 kids have amblyopia ("lazy eye" disease), which can lead to blindness, but the parents refuse to take the kids to an ophthalmologist; the 6-year-old is anemic, because his mother gives him too much milk, despite warnings from the pediatrician; all 3 kids have dental disease, including the baby who has "bottle rot", yet the parents refuse to do anything about it; the kids have dirty faces; they have no health insurance, because the mother refuses to get State insurance for them ("Husky" in Connecticut); and the parents totally minimize the kids' medical problems.

Why haven't the parents been arrested? It's enough to make your blood boil.

The problem is that none of it was true. And it took the parents, Jake and Freida, 21 months of aggravation and thousands of dollars in legal fees to clear their names. And no, they have not received an apology or reparations from CPS.

What happened is that the parents regularly took the children to a medical office that had half a dozen physicians, and then regularly saw, say, Dr. Smith or Dr. Jones. This day, however, neither physician was available, so they were assigned to, say, Dr. Brown.

Dr. Brown was a female physician and new to the office. She misread prior medical reports (just as lawyers can misread court documents). She saw at once that the parents were uneducated and lower-middle-class, and thus assumed that they must be indifferent to their children's needs. She began badgering the parents to do certain things, and when they refused, she called CPS.

ASIDE. One of the incredible things in this country is that everyone assumes that they are fair and balanced while others are prejudiced. I had a law school professor from Mississippi who swore to me that every time he opened his mouth with a Southern accent, people assumed he was uneducated and uncultured. As Frederick Loewe wrote in My Fair Lady, a "verbal class distinction." Someone even expressed surprise upon hearing that he and his wife went to the opera.

When I was about 10 years old, I figured out that the better-looking, more athletic, and taller kids had an advantage in the world. I didn't understand it but assumed I would when I got older. Now, about once every 5 years, I see a newspaper article saying that some college professor did a study and "discovered" that taller and better-looking persons had an advantage in the business world. It makes me smile for weeks.

Admit it. We all make pre-judgments before we have the facts, which is the literal Latin meaning of "prejudice." That's just what Dr. Brown did; the woman who couldn't be bothered to first check with the boys' regular doctors.

Here's a test. Suppose I show you a picture of two people. One is an adorable 7-year-old freckle-faced girl. The other is a 60-year-old man, bald, with a beard, and a leering look in his eye. I ask you which one is the child molester.

The correct answer is "I don't know." But I think we know how most of the public would answer.

In this case, the older man was a very popular Superior Court Judge who just happened to have that look. He was a solid citizen. The cute kid, my court-appointed client, was a sex pervert who went after younger children.

It would surprise most people to know that we have special regimented schools for child sex offenders, adolescent and younger. That's not something Americans like to think about, and you seldom see it on TV or in the movies. Producers won't show people what they don't want to see. But this adorable child was molested when younger, and that's what became of her.

After Dr. Brown's referral, CPS showed up at the door, unannounced. Among other things, the worker asked the boys if they had ever been "touched in bad places." That's when the parents lost it and screamed at the worker.

It was enough to prejudice the worker against the parents. She "substantiated" them for 12 offenses (each parent had 2 substantiations for each of the 3 boys).

ASIDE: A "substantiation" is a non-court, non-public notice that a parent has done something bad. It stays on their CPS record and can be used against them later. It can sometimes lead to being publicly placed on the Child Abuse Registry.

Jake and Freida finally called a lawyer. But he was a criminal lawyer, unschooled in CPS law. At least he was good enough to admit that he was out of his depth. Then they found me.

I filed for a CPS substantiation hearing and then researched the case thoroughly. Here is what the admitted evidence at the hearing revealed:

1. An optometrist with 32 years of experience testified that the kids did not have lazy eye. Although an M.D. had diagnosed one kid with 20/50 vision, in truth it was 20/25 uncorrected. How could an M.D. get it wrong? The optometrist testified that M.D.'s typically look to surgery, while optometrists look to treatment; and no surgery was required in this case. The optometrist further testified that lazy

eye does not necessarily lead to blindness; the social worker had simply "heard that somewhere" and included it in a legal document! He concluded that all 3 kids were doing well, visually.

2. A different pediatric ophthalmologist (M.D.) wrote a letter (acceptable at these hearings) stating that there was nothing remarkable in the kids' eye exams, and that any surgery would be cosmetic only.

3. A pediatric dentist with 31 years of experience testified that while one kid had tooth decay, it was impossible to tell the cause; and there was certainly no evidence of abuse or neglect. He added that the other kids were fine, the parents brought them in regularly, and he saw no problems. He politely disagreed with another dentist who had said that the kids were a "dental disaster." He hinted that the other dentist was somewhat hysterical and one who liked to drum up business.

4. Dr. Smith, one of the boys' regular pediatricians, testified that the kids were up to date medically, the mother was always cooperative, and that she never "minimized" problems.

5. Dr. Jones, the other regular pediatrician, testified similarly. Remarkably enough, neither Dr. Smith nor Dr. Jones even knew that CPS had been called on the family! Remarkable, but par for the course, is that CPS did not interview Drs. Jones or Smith.

6. The CPS social worker who took over the case after the initial "investigation" testified that the family was always cooperative, the home was well-kept, and no one minimized anything.

That was the admitted evidence. I omitted two extraneous facts. The optometrist (para 1 above) was so angry at CPS that he testified free of charge. The dentist (para 3 above) also testified free of charge. These facts restore one's faith in human goodness. Of course, the newspapers would never pick up any of these facts.

The CPS Hearing Officer made the rather obvious decision and reversed all 12 substantiations. Jake and Freida were cleared without having to go to court.

This case might have been lost had the optometrist and dentist, outraged at CPS's conduct, not volunteered their time. These professionals are true public heroes but will get no statues or other rewards.

I never did find out if Dr. Brown was chastised or fired. I filed no complaint against her. That was probably lazy and irresponsible of me, but I knew it would go nowhere. She would of course use the mandated reporting laws and say that she acted in good faith. True enough, but her laziness in not even talking to the regular doctors was certainly irresponsible at best.

We are all victims of our own prejudices. There are no exceptions, although some try harder than others to overcome this. As an exercise, try listing your own prejudices. You may be surprised.

Imagine if you were a good couple with three kids, and suddenly a State official came to your door and asked your kids if you had sexually abused them? We Americans love to talk about the lack of freedom in North Korea. True, we have it better here. But how much better?

CHAPTER 6: THE SPCA TO THE RESCUE

There are hundreds of more stories, and thousands on the internet, some even reflecting well on CPS. We'll tell a few later, but for now, you get the idea. At this point a little history is in order. How did we get to CPS in the first place?

As mentioned earlier, parents had life and death power over their children in the ancient world. There was no such thing as "protecting children from their parents", just as "protecting wives from their husbands" was unheard of.

All cultures, and even animals, recognize that the young need adult guidance. But what happens when a child becomes an orphan? Apparently not much in the ancient world, if we believe Homer. In Book 22 of the Iliad, after Hector is killed by Achilles, Hector's widow Andromache bewails the fate of their infant son Astyanax. In lines 485-505, Andromache paints a tear-jerking picture of Astyanax' being shunned, humiliated, and facing a life of complete sorrow just for being fatherless. We may assume that Homer was reflecting on the attitude of the times.

Then consciousness changed. The Old Testament has some references to the Lord warning people to not take advantage of widows and orphans, and exhorting people to protect the helpless (Isa. 1:17, Zech. 7:10). The New Testament also repeats this advice (James 1:27). The Catholic Church founded orphanages as early as the first century A.D., called "orphanotropia."

Fast forward. The English workhouses of the 19th century, so demonized by Charles Dickens and others, actually started as charitable efforts to assist orphans and abandoned children in the slums. There were of course people who took advantage of children. But there were also sincere, reform-minded persons who wanted to protect defenseless children, in an age when there were no meaningful guidelines for doing so.

Orphans were sometimes hired out to work in "respectable" families to pay for their upkeep, and also to learn the ways of the "productive" world. This situation is romanticized in James Whitcomb Riley's famous poem Little Orphant Annie, written in dialogue, and popular to this day through the comics and musicals.

Of course, even children who are not orphans may require services such as food, medical care, psychological counseling, and other protections that their guardians cannot or will not obtain. Charities developed. Slowly, the idea of government welfare for these unfortunates took shape. The social work profession started to develop. [There are books and articles available for those who wish to research the history of child welfare in depth].

However, there was no concept of protection specifically for abused children. In the early 20th Century in New York City, a social worker discovered a mother who was abusive even by the standards of the day. She was repeatedly abusing her daughter, even stabbing her with scissors; but under the law nothing could be done about it. And universal public sentiment was that family business was family business, period. But like an innovative lawyer, she found a way around it. She invoked provisions of the existing animal cruelty laws that had been passed due to pressure from the SPCA! This worker urged the Legislature to afford children the same protection as animals.

And thus began the idea that the government could, maybe, do something to protect abused or neglected children.

To be fair, there were early cases in America in which children had been removed from their parents by the courts, but they were very few and far between. For example, Connecticut enacted a law in 1881 allowing Justices of the Peace to commit a boy under the age of 16 to reform school if he were being brought up "to lead an idle or vicious life." One parent challenged this, but the State Supreme Court upheld the law in 1883.

The Great Depression began in 1929 and of course resulted in FDR's election. That resulted in the New Deal and the famous Social Security Act. A little-known provision of the Social Security Act was to provide federal grants to states for child welfare services. This obviously boosted the number of, and prestige of, social workers. Still, child welfare was largely akin to charity.

There used to be a successful crime and horror genre of comic books that featured extreme violence and sexual suggestions. I remember it well. All this changed in 1954, when Dr. Fredric Wertham published Seduction of the Innocent. This book led to Congressional hearings. While Wertham did exaggerate some of his criticisms, the end result was the abolition of certain successful comic lines and the adoption of a more stringent code for the comics. People were suddenly concerned about their effect on teenage and younger kids, although no one used the term "child abuse."

That changed almost overnight in 1962, when Dr. C. Henry Kempe published an article entitled "The Battered Child Syndrome" in the prestigious Journal of the American Medical Association. According to Dr. John M. Leventhal of Yale-New Haven Children's Hospital, Dr. Kempe's article "changed [child abuse] from a purely social problem into both a social and medical issue [and was] credited with raising both public and professional awareness of child abuse." The article also led to what are today called "mandatory reporting laws."

It also led to Congressional inquiries and the development of federal standards for child abuse protocols. Every State soon thereafter established a formal child protection agency. The social work profession became firmly established in America. Today you can even get Masters' and Doctoral degrees in social work.

Therefore, when we say "CPS," we refer to the child protective services system. CPS is administered by an agency in each State, under general guidelines (and funding) established by the federal Department of Health and Human Services (HHS). All of which is largely the result of Dr. Kempe's article. Connecticut started its CPS in 1969 as DCYS (Department of Children and Youth Services), later changing the name to DCF (Department of Children and Families).

It is still difficult to believe that when President Kennedy was elected, there was virtually no concept of protecting children from abuse or neglect in this country. I was a young adult by then.

Now the State had to help not only orphans, but also abused and neglected children. Orphanages were going out of style, although there are some left, and State-run homes don't seem much better. Thus, the little-used idea of foster care blossomed.

Two social work themes developed. One was to try to turn parents into suitable caregivers by offering services, such as parenting lessons, substance abuse treatment and counseling, domestic violence counseling, etc. The second was to place the children in licensed foster homes, temporarily or possibly permanently, if the parents did not respond properly.

These are excellent ideas, but as with all government programs, you never know when to stop. The feds, in granting money to states, conditioned those grants with the requirement that the agencies report the number of kids who were candidates for removal. As you might imagine, State agencies went where the money was, and more and more kids were removed form their homes. Needless to say, kids removed tended to be from poorer homes, with parents who had little or no resources to fight the State.

Happily, in the late 1970's, Congress got wind of the fact that too many kids were being removed from their homes. Hearings were held. In 1980 Congress passed legislation to provide a better balance between family stability and foster care. The major result – no surprise – was to require more paperwork, called "Treatment Plans." These are not a bad thing, but at least in Connecticut they are duplicative of already existing procedures.

People still could not make up their minds if enough kids were being removed, or if too many kids were being removed. There were various schools of thought: some people were upset that white kids were being placed with black families; others were upset that black kids were placed with white families; and still others were upset that there weren't enough interracial placements. Also, too many Indian kids were being removed, so laws were passed setting stricter standards for removing Indian kids. Yes, in equal opportunity America; and no one dared complain. The back-and-forth continues to this day.

But what were the limits of parents' rights? This was settled, apparently, in the somewhat bizarre 2000 U.S. Supreme Court case called Troxel v. Granville.

Most grandparents love their grandkids and want to see them as often as possible. Most parents know this and use the grandparents as free babysitters.

But not one certain family in Washington State. The parents decided that the grandparents could not see the kids.

The grandparents sued in state court and won limited visitation rights. The parents appealed, and it would up in the U.S. Supreme Court. The Court ruled that the 14th Amendment has a "privileges and immunities" clause. Under that clause, parents have a fundamental Constitutional right to oversee the care, custody, and control of their children.

Perhaps it was not nice to exclude the grandparents, but they had the right to do it.

In practice, this means that parents or guardians can do what they want, provided that they have an "intact family". "Intact family" means, is essence, that there are no reasonable allegations of abuse or neglect that would allow for CPS involvement.

So, if all is well, then control of the kids is up to the parents.

This brings us back to the old Roman law, but with modern protections for abused or neglected kids.

Consider if that early NYC social worker had agreed with the overwhelming prevailing thought that how you raised your kids was no one else's business. What if she had refused to argue and refused, like Dale Carnegie and his followers, to tell others that they were wrong? What if her husband had persuaded her to mind her own business and just collect her pension some day? Sooner or later we would have gotten a child protection system. But it is remarkable how one noble person's actions can speed things up; things that we take for granted today.

CHAPTER 7: JUNE IS BLOSSOMING

After high school I began college but busted out. I served three years in the Army, narrowly missing service in Vietnam. Then I graduated college with a B.A. in English Literature, from the University of Hartford, and went to work in an insurance company as a Programmer/Analyst. Let's just say that the bureaucratic life was not for me, but it was a good living. Finally I had had enough, and went to law school. I earned a J.D. magna cum laude from UConn Law (University of Connecticut School of Law).

I began as a solo lawyer in 1989, doing grunt work such as misdemeanor criminal defense, real estate, small business formation, wills, collections, and the like. In between the county [Judicial District in Connecticut] civil court and the criminal court was a building housing the CPS regional office and the Juvenile Court. [Today, the CPS office is elsewhere, and the Court has a different building of its own]. I struck up a conversation with the Juvenile Court clerk, a great lady named June. She asked me if I would like to take a few state-paid cases in Juvenile Court to supplement my income. I said yes, but that I knew nothing about it. She replied that I would learn. As I soon discovered, they were hard-up for state-paid lawyers, as the pay was pretty bad, and expense reimbursement almost non-existent.

June and I remained friends until the day she retired. She was a salt-of-the-earth civil servant; excellent and selfless.

One anecdote. A time came when I told June that I was swamped and couldn't take any more CPS cases for a month or so. But a week later she called me into her office and explained that there was a state-paid case with a very difficult father. He hated blacks, he hated women, and he distrusted younger people. "Frankly," she said, "I don't know who else to assign." I owed her a favor, so I took the case. Yes, he was difficult, but we got through it.

In any new field, you begin by watching the more experienced people. It was quite an education. CPS defense consisted of this:

When your client was an adult, you met them for the first time in court, told them to do whatever CPS said, and then disappeared until the next court hearing.

When your client was a kid named in a CPS petition, you met them for the first time in court, asked how they were, and then disappeared until the next court hearing.

You almost never challenged CPS written filings or actively contested a case by researching, summoning witnesses, and gathering documents.

You almost never called the social worker or their supervisor (or higher) to question an action or a decision, or offer your own views. The workers had free rein over the clients; lawyer or no lawyer.

If by any chance the client got your phone number and called and left a message, it was almost never returned.

Clients were never prepared for psychological evaluations, which are examinations conducted and tests administered by a court-appointed forensic clinical psychologist. Clients would go into these frightened, and very often flubbed the evaluations; resulting in dire consequences. Psych evals are discussed in detail later on.

Meeting clients in their homes was rare. Meeting clients in their homes when CPS was there was unheard-of. Advising clients before they signed CPS papers was considered unnecessary.

Defending clients in non-court administrative matters, such as Child Abuse Registry placements, was almost non-existent.

It didn't take long to see that CPS and their lawyers were used to getting their own way. It also didn't take long to see that CPS defense lawyers had a rather cavalier attitude toward their job. I knew that that was not the way to go.

But what was I doing special? Really, nothing. No defense that I ever conducted would have surprised a real criminal or civil lawyer. Reading pleadings and documentary evidence carefully, questioning, listening to your clients, researching, assembling witnesses and your own documentary evidence, getting experts, filing motions, planning cross examinations, etc., are all part of standard defense litigation.

So why were standard defense litigation skills so lacking in most CPS defense lawyers? As mentioned earlier, there was the lousy pay. But also, the field of CPS defense has not been established long enough to be taken seriously by most lawyers. Connecticut CPS started in 1969, and similar times in other states. Family protection law simply does not have the tradition of criminal law, divorce law, personal injury law, and almost every other kind of law.

Nowadays, the good CPS defense lawyers do perform the necessary work. But they are few and far between.

I once tried to start a national group of CPS defense lawyers and was politely told to get lost. The lawyers weren't interested. They saw nothing to gain by it.

A Connecticut Judge, who was a court administrator, once convened a committee to raise the bar for CPS defense lawyers. I was honored to be on the committee. We made several recommendations. Then the Judge retired. A few months later, I asked his successor about the recommendations. He told me curtly to forget it.

It's that kind of job. Makes you appreciate the good ones even more.

ASIDE. I've seen some parents hire top-flight criminal or divorce lawyers for Juvenile Court. That works only if the lawyer understands CPS and is experienced in it. The motions, procedures, practices, customs, discovery, standards of proof, and other legal niceties are quite different in Juvenile Court.

CHAPTER 8: THE INVESTIGATION FROM HELL

Ellie was a high school social worker dedicated to her job. One day she caught a student named Irving stealing a laptop computer from another teacher's room. Irving, a perennial troublemaker, was expelled. That should have ended the matter.

However, Irving's mother, Minnie, was a well-known local big mouth. She inveigled three of Irving's friends to make the following charges against Ellie:

She encouraged kids to smoke pot, on the theory that it made them better able to concentrate in class;

She was hiding pot in her classroom for the students;

She was giving students passes to go off grounds and smoke pot;

She was encouraging kids to steal so that they could buy pot;

Best of all, she was allowing kids to make drug deals in her office.

Minnie took that "evidence" and complained to the school. The authorities searched Ellie's room and found nothing.

Minnie complained to the police. They investigated and closed the matter with no charges.

Minnie called the State's Attorney (D.A.). He also investigated and found nothing.

Undaunted, Minnie started a social media campaign against Ellie, defaming her in front of the entire community. That resulted in a lawsuit which was eventually settled out of court. Note that it never occurred to Minnie that she was enabling her own son's criminal behavior; really good training for adulthood.

You would think this was enough, but Minnie was as stubborn as I am. She now played her trump card: she called CPS. CPS of course assigned an investigator to the case. But that investigator turned out to be an old pal of Minnie's from high school, and he found the charges to be true! He did not recuse himself from the case!!

On that basis, CPS recommended that Ellie be placed on the Child Abuse Registry, which would have barred her from any school jobs for life.

Following normal procedure, Ellie went to her Union rep. They and their lawyers were in way over their heads, knowing nothing about CPS but refusing to admit it. Fortunately, Ellie caught on and found our firm.

ASIDE. There seems to be a custom in America that you can never admit that you don't know something. It is better to be wrong than to admit you don't know and refer the caller to someone who may know. This is fertile ground for psychological or sociological research.

So I got the case, noting that there was absolutely no physical or background evidence against Ellie. In fact, all of her professional colleagues gave her high marks. The only "evidence" against her was the word of four juvenile delinquents.

A CPS Administrative Registry Hearing was scheduled. It turned out that since the "witnesses" were juveniles, they were considered victims and could not be called to testify under CPS admin hearing rules!! Therefore, I threatened to file a motion to have their Juvenile Court and school records given to the Hearing Officer as evidence. That got CPS to formally admit that all their witnesses were delinquent kids.

And there was more. I found out that the investigator had spoken to the mother of one of the kids, but that mother spoke no English! The investigator refused to say who the interpreter was; but almost certainly, it was her kid himself. Can you believe? I mean, really.

Also, the investigator, in his report recommending the Registry, paid no credence to Ellie's sterling record, and refused to speak to the Principal, school security officers, and other teachers who would have supported Ellie. For added measure, he introduced a text message unfavorable to Ellie, while neglecting to show a text message sent two minutes later that indicated the exact opposite. Quite a Prince.

This was a "case" like no other. I can think of absolutely no reason for the investigator's incredible behavior other than his long-standing friendship with Minnie.

I would like to tell you that the investigator was later disciplined, but he retired shortly after this "case" was over.

I took all my findings to the CPS in-house lawyer who would be trying the case. I explained that she would make a fool out of herself by pushing this; and that if by some miracle we lost at the hearing, we would certainly win at a Superior Court appeal. I pushed hard because I didn't want Ellie to spend thousands of dollars over this nonsense.

It finally worked. CPS dropped the charges. Ellie is now a social worker at another school.

For years thereafter, Ellie kept sending me e-mails that I had saved her life, and there was nothing she could ever do to repay me. But her messages did exactly that.

It is common to read about corruption in the papers or see it on TV. Most people ask, "How could this happen?" The better question is "Why don't you report more of it?" Corruption is so rampant in society that if we had newspapers and TV stations reporting nothing else, they would never run out of material.

And at the bottom of this investigator's malfeasance and total irresponsibility: good old corruption and laziness. I am just sorry to God above that he never got his due.

If you want to feel sorry for anyone, it's Minnie's son, whose mother set the "example" by which to lead his life.

CHAPTER 9: NOBODY LIKES TO LOSE

Everybody likes to win, but lawyers at least are expected to play by the rules. Aren't they?

Biff and Karen were a pleasant-enough young couple with three kids, living in a nice suburban neighborhood. Biff was a police officer and had a bit of a temper, however. After a domestic squabble (no physical violence), CPS filed a petition and got an order of protective supervision (PS) for 6 months. The couple figured out to hire us, and all was going well. They saw the required counselors and therapists, cooperated with the school, cooperated with CPS and the kids' lawyer, and all was going well.

At a pretrial conference, CPS agreed to end PS for the two younger kids. However, they wanted to extend it for 6 more months for the older kid. I convinced the CPS lawyer that this was nonsense, and she talked CPS out of it. A formal court hearing was set in two months to see if PS should end as scheduled.

However, when word got back to the CPS office manager, she was displeased that her workers had been talked out of extending PS.

About a month before the scheduled court hearing, I wrote to CPS and asked if all was well, and if anything had come up to change our agreement that PS would be ended. I sent three follow-ups and contacted the kids' lawyer, but strangely got no response.

On the day of the hearing, CPS bagged us by filing a memo saying that it would move to extend PS, as the oldest kid remained "disturbed". The memo quoted the kid's psychiatrist, psychologist, and a teacher to that effect; seemingly quite a bit of evidence.

ASIDE. This kind of bagging is fortunately no longer allowed. CPS now has to give advance notice to the parents' lawyer. Even without that requirement, it was one of the shabbiest of all courtroom tricks. I am surprised that the CPS lawyer went along with it, and that she never checked out the "facts" quoted in the memo.

What CPS thought of me, I cannot imagine. But I personally contacted the psychiatrist, psychologist, and the teacher, and all said that the kid was fine and that CPS should be out of the picture now. In fact, the psychologist "quoted" by CPS said that CPS had never even spoken to him!

I subpoenaed all these witnesses into court and wrote a blistering memo attacking CPS's good faith. The kid's lawyer supported us.

On the day of the court hearing, CPS saw the witnesses standing in the hallway and immediately backed down, without a trial. It was a total settlement, without even the benefit of a pre-trial conference.

You seldom see that on Law and Order.

It is frightening to contemplate what could have happened. CPS could have driven this couple crazy, to the point where Biff would really have lost his temper ("See; we told you!"). And of course the couple had to expend sums of money for nothing; just to placate a manager's vindictiveness. I should have filed a formal complaint against the CPS worker for her false memo, and against the CPS lawyer for not checking the facts in their pleading; but I knew it would come to nothing. We are protecting children, after all.

I once had a very liberal judge, a Democrat stalwart, tell me privately that CPS workers sometimes had to push the envelope, because parents often lie. Could you imagine him saying that the police should beat confessions out of criminal suspects "to get at the truth"?

~~~

Not only does CPS not like to lose, but children do not either. I have had cases where kids as young as nine years old complained to their teachers that their parents were abusing them. This required the teachers, as mandated reporters, to call CPS. Most times, this "abuse" turned out to be grounding them from their phones or computers. Several cases featured teenage boys complaining on behalf of their "abused" girlfriends, when the parents did not want their daughter to see this particular boy. People who think kids are not that sophisticated are in another world. Kids learn the rules, they talk, and the surefire tricks get around.

A friend of mine who teaches in a middle school told me that they have kids who read the Student Handbook and say, "OK, so this is what I have to do to get thrown out. Otherwise you can't touch me."

It's one thing to care about kids' rights. But you must remember that kids have few responsibilities and little experience, and can and do easily abuse those rights. Yet that matters little to CPS, which sees its statistics growing.

Please do not ever wonder why we are raising a generation of entitled, work-averse, non-productive citizens. It all starts with the parents. You cannot delegate parenting to the State.

I'll say one thing for my own mom. She never bought this "all the other kids are doing it" nonsense.

"It takes a village to raise a child" is a wonderful phrase intended solely as a rationale for avoiding parental responsibility. And this is called "Progressive."

Edgar Lee Masters put it best, as his character "Lucinda Matlock" speaks in *Spoon River Anthology*:

> *What is this I hear of sorrow and weariness,*
> *Anger, discontent and drooping hopes?*
> *Degenerate sons and daughters,*
> *Life is too strong for you –*
> *It takes life to love life.*

CHAPTER 10: "EQUITY REGARDS AS DONE…."

We will consider a true CPS deadly disaster in the next chapter. But first, some background.

One of my law professors was the late great Cornelius J. Scanlon. Neil, as his friends called him, was the most beloved member of the faculty. He had a saying in Contract Law: "Equity regards as done that which ought to be done."

So doesn't everybody want to do equity? This is as good a time as any to consider the most emotional of the modern acronyms: DEI. It plays a role in CPS cases.

"D" stands for diversity, or a work force that consists of different ethnic groups, races, genders, sexualities, religions, and the like. "I" stands for inclusion, meaning that diversity itself is not sufficient; the diverse populations must all be made to feel welcomed and comfortable. "E" stands for equity, meaning that you may hire and promote someone other than the most qualified person, in order to make up for past injustices.

Opponents of DEI say that hiring and promoting less-qualified people is patently unfair. Proponents of DEI say that there are plenty of incompetent white male heterosexual native-born Protestant managers and executives, so why shouldn't minorities get a share of the pie? With the incompetence that I have seen in business and government, this argument strikes a chord.

Proponents of DEI also point out the obvious injustices done to blacks in this country. Opponents point out that other groups also suffered prejudice, although not as bad, and they managed to break through.

It is important to understand where DEI came from. Fortunately, I was in at the start and can explain.

It is obvious that the U.S. has always had prejudice and discrimination. Not as obvious is that all societies have had prejudices against minorities. The U.S. has at least acknowledged the problem and done something about it.

When Jews were not allowed in country clubs, they started their own country clubs. When Jews were denied staff privileges at Hartford Hospital, they started Mount Sinai Hospital. The Irish, Italians, Asians, Indians and numerous other ethnic groups also managed to reasonably integrate into American society.

However, it was not the same for the blacks. There are many possible reasons for this, and I am not attempting to write a sociology textbook. I just note the obvious. In doing so, I reject the idea of so-called "systemic racism." This theory says that whites plot against blacks, consciously or unconsciously. While there certainly are whites who hate blacks (or Jews, Catholics, Protestants, Asians, Muslims, etc.), most whites that I know are too busy trying to make a living to hold planning sessions on how to keep the blacks down.

ASIDE. I personally believe that the reason for lack of total black assimilation is the vote-buying welfare system that encourages single parenthood and thus the destruction of families. However, I realize this is an emotional issue, and I have probably made enough enemies by now. Just look at the illegitimacy statistics if you are in doubt.

Therefore, in the 60's and 70's, the idea of Affirmative Action took hold. At the insurance company, it worked like this. Suppose you wanted to hire 10 computer programmers. You advertised, and people applied, some qualified, some not. Of the 10 people you hired, 2 had to be black, provided that at least 2 blacks were among the qualified applicants. Also, 3 of the hires had to be women, provided that at least 3 women were among the qualified applicants. The idea was to keep up this practice until senior management deemed that the problem of past discrimination had ended.

As thus understood, affirmative action made sense, at least to me. However, it was never "thus understood." There were at least three major problems:

1. Why should the protected groups include only blacks and women? What about homosexuals, physically challenged (which used to be called handicapped), transsexuals (this came later), fat people,

homely people, short people, autistic people, Muslims, Asians, Sikhs, and others? They could point to past discrimination also.

2. When will discrimination "end?" Clearly, never. Have you ever known anyone who willingly gave up a special economic privilege? And if you said that discrimination was over, someone could always point to an isolated incident to "prove" that it wasn't.

3. How will this affirmative action be implemented? Suppose a manager says that he cannot find 2 qualified blacks or 3 qualified women. In practice, he will be told that he hasn't tried hard enough. The affirmative action "goals" will be put in his file. He quickly understands that even though they are not stated to be quotas, they actually are. It's one thing for policy wonks to say "There are no quotas. You have to try harder". But it's quite another for line managers whose bread and butter is at stake.

The result, of course, is that affirmative action became an unworkable joke. This happened doubly at the insurance company, when women who supervised clerical units were counted as "Managers", despite the fact that they made less money than computer programmers, who were classified as merely "Technical." But everyone knew that you had to go along to get along.

Gradually, affirmative action became widely recognized as a disguised quota system, so Diversity was substituted for it. "Our strength is our diversity" became the standard slogan. No one knew quite what that meant, but no worries: diversity "consultants" appeared out of the woodwork to explain it, drawing hefty fees that sometimes bordered on extortion. Books were written and seminars held. No qualifications other than being a minority were needed.

And then Inclusion. No one could ever feel "threatened." There was still bullying against weak persons, of course, as a normal part of corporate work. But no statements that might even arguably or unreasonably suggest racial or homophobic or religious overtones (except against Christians) were allowed. That is where the thought police came in. People became afraid to speak, except in whispered tones to their closest friends. E-mail became a vehicle to be feared. Unlucky persons were fired or demoted or cancelled. Even comedians felt unsafe doing what had been standard comedy and parody. America became a joyless nation.

Totally innocent white people were made to attend seminars in which they had to admit their guilt and shame at being born white. V.M. Hillyer described the craziness of the Terror after the French Revolution as "people gone wild, crazy, mad." This is a perfectly apt description of the effects of so-called inclusion. God be thanked; I was a lawyer by that time.

I'll never forget going to my granddaughter's holiday concert when she was in middle school. They sang "Winter Wonderland" at one point, and this phrase was sung:

> In the winter we can build a snowman
> And pretend that he is such a clown…

Of course, the correct verse is "Parson Brown." But that "religious reference" might have offended someone!

But diversity and inclusion were not enough. Apparently not enough minorities were yet in high positions. So equity came into being as the answer to correcting past wrongs. As mentioned earlier, there were plenty of incompetent "majority" people, but hiring and promoting incompetent minority people was hardly the answer to the problem. (Education and common sense were the answer, but no one was interested in those relics).

On colleges, segregated dorms and graduations were somehow seen as fostering equity.

ASIDE. Some will wonder why large corporations embraced diversity in the first place. These are businesses that care only about the bottom line and are generally not customer friendly. I believe that the whole thing was a ruse dreamed up by P.R. people to cuddle up to Democrats, so they could have allies in both parties. Also, it served as a marketing gimmick. I have seen very little in corporations or government agencies that is "equitable."

This is the milieu that President Trump was referring to when he ordered that DEI be abolished in the federal government. While some racists will cheer, the majority of the cheering will be done by all classes of people who favor common sense and competence in government and business.

To repeat the obvious: there will always be prejudice and discrimination. The answer is education, and the setting of examples by parents, community leaders, business leaders, and political leaders. The answer is not government quotas and seminars.

Of course, the ones screaming the loudest are the incompetent people themselves. Plus those making money as DEI "executives" and "consultants."

DEI then showed up in CPS defense. Some leftist lawyers started accusing CPS workers of being prejudiced against minorities. We shall see if this is true. The idea was to defund CPS, just as radicals after George Floyd wanted to defund the police; or at least sharply curtail it.

~~~

An anecdote from the Army.

In 1948, President Truman signed an executive order desegregating the military. Roosevelt could have done it but was afraid to, since he needed the support of powerful Southern Senators to pass the New Deal. Therefore, when I got to Germany in January 1963, the Army had been desegrated for only 15 years.

It didn't seem that way, however. Whites and blacks, and a few Asians, lived and worked together in harmony. I can't remember a serious racial incident in my 3 years. However, at Fort Gordon, I once heard a black sergeant shout at a bunch of redneck whites, "Don't you look at me that way! If we fight in Cuba, my blood will flow just as red as yours!" That was it.

We had one fellow in Germany named Lloyd. He was a West Virginia mountaineer type, and he made it quite clear that he didn't like blacks. He was a real tough guy, but he knew enough to tone it down to avoid an incident. Yet everyone knew where he stood.

It is unlikely that Lloyd had run into many blacks in the mountains. All he knew of them was through the media. So it shouldn't be that surprising that he feared them and hence hated them.

Somehow, Lloyd liked me, and we talked often. One day he said, "Well, Mac is OK," referring to one of the popular black soldiers. "He isn't like the others." Later on he added that Smitty, another black soldier, was a really good guy.

By the time I had mustered out, Lloyd was friendly with most of the black soldiers and hung around with them just like anybody else. I suspect he had found out, by living with blacks, that they had feelings and hopes and expectations just like whites. Some were good and some were bad, just like whites.

This, of course, is exactly what Dr. Martin Luther King understood when he marched for integration. He knew that more than working with people, living with them was the best cure for discrimination. He famously asked that people be judged by the content of their character, not the color of their skin. Believe me, no one had lectured Lloyd about prejudice or sent him to any seminars or focus groups on the subject. We didn't do that then.

It is disheartening to read about groups who want their own separate housing and graduations and safe spaces and classrooms. An uneducated mountain boy could have told them better. And the politicians who preach "diversity" while living in their gated and guarded communities are beneath contempt.

And Dr. King's admonition to judge people on the content of their character bears repeating, over and over again. It is true in all avenues of life, and you will never go wrong following it. The lowest person on the social scale may have superb character and teach you a few things.

~~~

I know that DEI still has many passionate defenders. If you are one of them, please take the time to read the Appendix. It details my own personal adventure into the world of DEI.

~~~

CHAPTER 11: HOW DEI HELPED TO KILL A CHILD

The American Bar Association runs a blog for CPS lawyers. A few years ago, DEI radicals took over the blog, insisting that CPS was nothing but a bunch of prejudiced goons who targeted blacks, Hispanics, and Native Americans. The blog moderator was intimidated. When I protested, I was told to "tone it down or get thrown off the list." This really happened in America. One lawyer even threatened to punch my lights out, and I just dared him to come up here and try it.

The Hartford Courant once ran an article stating that inner-city school Principals were concerned that kids were coming to school hungry. Nowhere did the article mention that the Principals had called CPS. If my granddaughter had come to school complaining that she was hungry, CPS would have been at her home in 5 minutes. I asked a CPS lawyer why inner-city parents got a break. She assured me that that was not the case. Really.

On August 19, 1999, a child named Matthew Tirado was born to a Hispanic woman in Hartford. On February 14, 2017, at age 17, he died. The mother was later arrested and imprisoned for manslaughter. It turned out, among other things, that she had starved the kid to death. Matthew's Estate wanted to sue CPS for wrongful death, saying that it had failed to protect Matthew when it had a duty to do so.

You cannot sue the State in this type of situation without its permission. After years of trying, in 2022, the Estate finally got permission from the State Claims Commissioner to file a lawsuit. On October 16, 2024, the case settled at pretrial, and the Estate was awarded $1.6 Million.

You can go to the Connecticut Judicial Department website and look up the case, Norsigian v. State of Conn., Docket No. HHD-CV-22-6161400-S. You can go to the Superior Court and ask to see the file. Or you can read the following timeline and decide for yourself.

** DATE	** EVENT
8/19/1999	Matthew is born
2/6/2006	CPS substantiates the mother for educational neglect, as Matthew had excessive absences from school
1/26/2007	CPS investigated mother for physical neglect of Matthew, but it was unsubstantiated
7/12/2007	Vickie, younger sister of Matthew, was born, of a different father
11/24/2014	CPS substantiated physical abuse of Vickie, age 7. She told her teacher that she was afraid to go home. Incredibly, CPS did NOT investigate regarding Matthew. It is standard that one sibling's possible abuse is ALWAYS cause for looking into the welfare of the other siblings. But not here.
12/1/2014	Educational neglect of Matthew was again substantiated
3/30/2015	CPS referred mother for a substance abuse screen and evaluation. She never attended. CPS did not pursue the matter.
5/15/2015	

46

	Educational neglect of Vickie was substantiated
8/16/2015	Mother made an appointment for a physical for Vickie, but did not show up
9/29/2015	Mother made another appointment for a physical for Vickie, but again did not show up. Vickie was later diagnosed with Global Development Delay
2/1/2016	Matthew had been attending the Oak Hill School. This was the last day he showed up.
3/14/2016	Mother told CPS that she was moving Matthew to his aunt's home in a nearby town, but did not provide CPS with any details. CPS subsequently observed Matthew to actually be at his Mother's home, but remarkably, did nothing.
3/28/2016	Mother did meet with CPS, but refused to meet with them after that. CPS, which knew that Matthew was autistic, was unable to determine if he was up-to-date medically and dentally, yet did nothing.
4/15/2016	Vickie's school reported concerns to CPS over her missed

	schooling. Mother refused to sign releases allowing CPS to contact the school. Following standard procedure, this would be an automatic red flag to file a Juvenile Court petition regarding Vickie; but it was not done.
7/1/2016	CPS finally filed a neglect petition regarding Matthew in the Juvenile Court. It alleged educational neglect and living under conditions injurious to his wellbeing.
8/9/2016	CPS recommended protective supervision (PS) for 6 months for Matthew. A court hearing was scheduled in one week for the Judge to decide.
8/16/2016	Mother was a no-show at court. The Judge ordered CPS to make good-faith efforts to find her. Inexplicably, no such order was given to Matthew's court-appointed lawyer to find Matthew. Case continued to 8/23/2016.
8/19/2016	Mother was reported as Hispanic. "Hispanic" is a protected class, per Connecticut DCF [CPS] Office of Equity and Diversity Policy 7-1. Connecticut DCF is committed to "affirmative

action" in administrative matters. Like all affirmative action, there is no doubt that there are no official quotas, but line workers and managers understand what it means. Further, Connecticut DCF was certainly aware of the previously mentioned agitation by leftist lawyers regarding DEI and social worker "bias", and wanted to avoid trouble at all cost.

8/23/2016	Mother still a no-show. Case continued to 9/13/2016.
9/13/2016	Mother still a no-show. Case continued to 9/27/2016. Judge threatened to issue a capias, or civil arrest order, for Mother.
9/27/2016	Mother still a no-show. Judge asked CPS if they still wanted to pursue the case, since they hadn't been able to locate the Mother. Incredibly, no one, including Matthew's lawyer, asked for a Bench OTC, which is an order of temporary custody to bring in Matthew, ordered by the Judge, who has that authority. It occurred to no one that Matthew might be in imminent danger, given the voluminous history of this case.

10/6/2016	Another court hearing. CPS stated that Mother was still in the area. The Judge asked if the primary issue was "educational neglect." CPS said yes. Matthew's lawyer, who should have known of probable physical danger, had NO COMMENT. There is no indication that that lawyer ever even tried to see the kid.
12/8/2016	Court hearing. A day that will live in infamy in the annals of Connecticut. CPS had reported two days prior that it had been extremely difficult to locate the Mother, so the case should end. The CPS lawyer at the hearing was a lady well-known to me as a real fighter. We had plenty of battles against each other in the past. Yet she just gave in. Matthew's "lawyer" uttered not one word of objection. The Juvenile Court case ended. NOTE: When I called Matthew's "lawyer" in 2024, he had the decency to admit that he was negligent, then hung up the phone. My wife persuaded me not to try to have him disbarred, which I believe is the least he deserves; if not jail time.

2/14/2017	Matthew dies
5/15/2017	Mother is arrested for Manslaughter. She had essentially been starving this autistic child and neglecting all of his physical needs.
6/5/2017	Mother sentenced to 17 years in prison, suspended after 11 years. Meanwhile, thank the Lord, Mother's parental rights to Vickie had been terminated, and Vickie was adopted by a good family.
9/11/2018	The newspapers pick up the story that Matthew's Estate filed for permission to sue the State of Connecticut [DCF] with the Claims Commissioner. I write to Matthew's law firm, a large, well-established firm that I know has no CPS experience, and offer my help. There the letter sits for years. It is not surprising that big firms often feel that they have nothing to learn from an unknown small lawyer.
10/7/2022	After years of wrangling, the Claims Commissioner grants permission for Matthew's Estate to sue CPS. A lawsuit is filed in Hartford Superior Court. The

	lead CPS lawyer fights like hell. They will not give in. Motion after motion, depositions, etc. CPS absolutely will not admit to its obvious negligence. Clearly, CPS is spending all its money to ensure that there will be little or no award to Matthew's Estate; which means Vickie in this case.
9/3/2024	Matthew's lawyers are discussing how to settle the case in their office, when suddenly the senior lawyer remembers a letter that he got years ago (9/11/18). An associate calls me, I agree to help, and she sends over the case file.
9/19/2024	Matthew's lawyers file a motion to depose me as an expert witness in the case. I sent my credentials to them. CPS already had an expert witness who testified that CPS had done nothing wrong. It was just a simple case of educational neglect that had an unfortunate turn. That "expert" was a "Certified Child Welfare Specialist", certified by the prestigious-sounding National Association of Counsel for Children. It turns out that "certification" requires a few years as a CPS lawyer, taking

some online courses (with no tests), getting letters from friends, and paying $400.00 plus periodic maintenance and recertification fees.

I countered with a lengthy list of what I had accomplished, with summaries of numerous cases.

The case settled for $1.6 Million. Vickie will have some money for college. Whether or not I had anything to do with it cannot be determined with certainty. But it is reasonably certain that if I had gotten involved in 2018, the case would have settled faster.

There is not even a colorable argument that this case was about anything other than DEI. CPS certainly had its "Hispanic quota" for the year and wasn't going to pursue this case. This, despite the fact that the red flags were a lot more serious than many of the cases mentioned elsewhere in this essay.

It is of course possible that someone made a mistake. But it is not possible that the social worker, social work supervisor, program manager, CPS Area Director, CPS in-house lawyer, CPS outside counsel, and Matthew's lawyer, all made the identical mistake under these facts. That is less likely than a false DNA match.

As noted, Matthew's lawyer was at least gracious enough to admit his negligence to me privately. I hope to Heaven he is more attentive to his own kids.

So, to those leftist lawyers who argue that CPS is biased against minorities, be aware that it is the other way around.

The irresponsibility shown by CPS (and the child's lawyer) resulted in the death of an innocent autistic child, and a substantial loss to the taxpayers of Connecticut. And no one was disbarred or went to jail, other than the mother whom CPS had let off the hook.

I have repeatedly and vehemently urged CPS to get rid of DEI practices. I hope to God it happens.

Finally, I am aware that CPS defenders will say that this case was just an unlucky accident. Sorry, but I can't buy it. There were too many highly improbable events to make Matthew's death just a sad coincidence. I know how affirmative action "non quotas" work, and this was one of them.

To be fair, the State Child Advocate argued that it was all a home schooling problem. If there had been "better controls" on kids taken out of public schools, the problem would have been avoided.

Home schooling advocates complained that they were being unfairly targeted.

The State's position seems to have some validity, but it is actually without merit. CPS had plenty of cause and opportunity to investigate the situation. And it seems unreasonable to have overworked teachers, in this day of declining test scores, acting effectively as unpaid CPS supervisory agents.

The Child Advocate's position was basically throwing a bone to the anti-home-schooling lobby. Matthew deserved better.

CHAPTER 12: WE WILL PSYCH YOU OUT

In a trial, witnesses state the facts within their knowledge. They do not give their opinions except in very limited circumstances. But there can be "expert witnesses" who are allowed to give their opinions. In a criminal trial, it is common to have fingerprint experts, blood spatter experts, ballistics experts, etc. In a civil trial, it is common to have engineers and accident reconstruction experts, etc.

In a CPS trial, you also have experts. These are primarily forensic clinical psychologists. Sometimes you have psychiatrists, but rarely. The clinical psychologists are the people who supposedly know what makes you tick and can predict how you are likely to react in the future.

ASIDE. For a good popular discussion of the fascinating field of psychology from the beginning of time to the present, see The Story of Psychology, by Morton Hunt. For a more scholarly discussion by an expert in the field, noting the limits of the field and criticizing some of its claims, read Science and Pseudoscience in Clinical Psychology, Scott O. Lilienfeld, ed.

So clinical psychologists are the experts who advise the Judge in matters such as:

Should the kids be removed from the parents?

If the kids are removed, should they later be returned to the parents?

If returned to the parents, what protections should be in place?

If the kids cannot be returned to the parents, should there be a TPR?

The clinical psychologists are, needless to say, a very important part of the Juvenile Court process.

In most cases, the Court appoints a clinical psychologist. It orders the parents (and possibly other adults, or even the kids) to have a psychological evaluation.

In almost all such cases this scares the parents half to death. They assume they are going to a CPS psychologist and will be examined and possibly tricked. They have no idea what to say or do. A poor evaluation result can mean disaster,

Everyone believed at first that the psychologists were court-appointed and neutral. But were they?

I discovered, to my amazement, that that was not originally the case. The Connecticut psychologists were actually contracted by, reviewed by, and subject to dismissal by – ready – CPS! Thus, the court-appointed "neutral" experts were actually contractors of one of the parties to the case!! This is like an auto accident case in which the court appoints an "independent" accident reconstruction expert who is actually on the payroll of either the plaintiff or the defendant.

Note: I had never suspected this. I discovered it by accident in the course of a routine inquiry.

I brought this anomaly to the attention of the Connecticut CPS Commissioner and the Chief CPS Legal Officer at a meeting. They assured me that there was no problem. I said sorry, but it would have to be changed. The Chief Legal Officer, a good lady and a good friend, laughed in my face and said, "No way!"

I wrote to the Attorney General of Connecticut, Richard Blumenthal. He is now the Senior United States Senator from Connecticut. At the time, as Connecticut AG, he was technically in charge of the Assistant Attorneys General (AAG's) who argued in court as CPS lawyers.

I had a lobbyist friend who had told me that a politician will never act unless he sees something in it for himself. That is, any action has to bring votes, money, or publicity. I believe that is true, but here was the one exception that proves the rule. AG Blumenthal actually wrote back to me that this was unfair, and that he would work to change it!

This was incredible. AG Blumenthal's actions could bring him no votes (who else cared?), no publicity (the papers don't generally run CPS stories), and certainly no money (except maybe a small contribution from me). Yet he did it because it was right. It was the most unselfish act I have ever seen in the political arena.

Still, it took one full year to implement this change. But it was accomplished. The Connecticut clinical psychologists are now retained and paid for by the courts and not by CPS. I resisted the temptation to call my Legal Officer friend and razz her.

And by the way: I found out from a few courageous psychologists that CPS actually did apply subtle pressure to psychologists who didn't come up with the "right" opinion often enough. They didn't fire them outright, but they saw to it that they weren't appointed in enough cases by the courts.

Now the lawyer must tell the client what to expect. What really is a psychological evaluation?

It turns out not to be that difficult. The evaluation has five parts:

1. QUESTIONS TO BE ANSWERED.

There is no such thing as an evaluation in the abstract. The psychologist is given a list of questions to answer. Typical ones are: "What is the psychological functioning of the mother?"; "What would be the benefit (or harm) to the child if returned to the parents?"; "How likely is it that the father can rehabilitate from his alcohol problem, and what treatment would be needed?"; etc.

2. DOCUMENTS SUBMITTED

The psychologist gets reports telling them what the case is about and the general history of matters, so that they have a basis from which to start.

3. COLLATERAL CONTACTS

The psychologist is given a list of experts to call who have worked on the case. Releases are signed, and the psychologist can call them for their opinions.

4. INTERVIEW

The court arranges interviews between the psychologist and the parents. Other persons, such as the children, or even possibly other witnesses, may be interviewed also.

5. TESTING

The psychologist administers what are called "psychological testing instruments", or "psych tests" or "personality tests." These may be "objective tests" in which you answer "Yes/No" or, in more sophisticated versions, "Always/often/sometimes/never", etc. These may also be "subjective tests" in which there are no predefined answers. The most famous example is the Rorschach test, in which you are shown "ink blots" and asked to describe what you see. Others include reading a brief story or looking at a picture and describing what you see.

After the above steps are completed, the psychologist will prepare a psychological evaluation report. He or she answers the questions that were asked. This report is used as evidence in court. The psychologist, as an expert witness, may be examined or cross-examined on the report.

So, how can a CPS defense lawyer help the client?

1. QUESTIONS TO BE ANSWERED.

In former days, CPS simply prepared the questions. This was unfair to say the least. As the saying goes, "He who controls the questions controls the outcome." CPS accomplished this neat trick by ensuring that there was a set of "Standard Questions" on an official-looking form. But there was nothing "official" about it. It was merely CPS's list that no one had ever challenged! Well, we challenged it and often objected to CPS's questions and inserted some of our own. Thankfully, this has now become standard practice. If the lawyers cannot agree on the questions at their pre-trial conference, then the Judge decides.

2. DOCUMENTS SUBMITTED.

This one was fascinating. In Connecticut, there is a document called a "Summary of Facts", which is CPS's version of the facts and their interpretation. Nothing wrong with that, but as a piece of paper it is just hearsay. It is normally not admitted in court unless someone testifies about it and can be cross-examined. However, the Summary of Facts served one useful purpose: it was submitted to the psychologist as the "statement of the case." To say this was unfair is to gild the lily.

However, a little-known provision of the Practice Book (Court Rules) said that a lawyer could prepare a "Response to the Summary of Facts." Most lawyers never bothered, but we did. We insisted that it be given to the psychologist along with CPS Summary. This has now become, in most cases, standard practice.

For those who wonder: peer-reviewed studies have shown that even trained and experienced clinical psychologists can be subject to biases just like ordinary folks. They can be influenced by the first thing that they read and hear, and even their own past experiences. No one is immune. See Cross-Examining Experts in the Behavioral Sciences, Thompson/West Publishers. In other words, it is important to get your two cents in at the start.

3. COLLATERAL CONTACTS

If there were psychologists and therapists on our side, we ensured that these were also made available to the evaluator. One problem kept cropping up: the evaluator would often say that they had left messages for our people which were not returned. A good part of the job was nothing more than phone calls and e-mails to end this "communication problem." It was pure legal grunt work, but it had to be done and was done, with the help of excellent paralegals.

4. INTERVIEW

As mentioned, people undergoing a psych eval were nervous. Many would either clam up or babble on. We had to explain to them, using several examples, that you answer questions honestly and fully in 2-3 sentences. You don't ramble, which shows nervousness; and you don't act brusque, which shows an attempt to hide information.

We also told people how to dress for interviews, who to call if something went wrong, and a host of other things to put them at ease. Put it this way: no one who ever took my advice "flunked" a psych eval. After reading hundreds of psych evals, even a layman gets to know the gist.

5. TESTING

The standard objective test at the time was called the MMPI-2: Minnesota Multiphasic Personality Inventory, Version 2. (Hunt's book discusses this, and it is well worth reading). You answered questions with a "Yes" or "No", and each answer was fed into a computer which assigned it to one or more scales and subscales. For example, if you answered too many questions one way, you might be "elevated" or "highly elevated" on the Social Alienation Scale, the Hysteria Scale, the Lie scale (they are smart enough to check for inconsistent answers), the Antisocial Behavior Scale, etc. From the interview, collateral contacts, and testing results, bolstered by the Social Study and Response. the psychologist could answer the questions posed by the Court.

There are several books telling you all this. They would explain, for example, that answering Question #117 as "True" would get one tick on Scales A,C, and D, and Subscales D-1 and F-2. But there seemed to be no way to get the actual questions themselves! These were "state secrets"; actually, secrets for the use of licensed clinical psychologists only. I later found out, using a private detective in Washington, D.C., that you couldn't even get the questions from the Library of Congress!

As mentioned, sometimes subjective tests such as the ink-blot test were used. Many psychologists swore by them; others thought they were one step above voodoo. I discovered from available books that the test results did not depend solely on what you answered. They also considered how long you looked at each drawing, and whether you tried to turn it around before answering. Needless to say, the clients were advised of this also.

I did not, and still do not, consider this cheating. To me, it is leveling the playing field for people who are scared to death and have a lot at stake; to wit, the custody of their children.

We found some ways to challenge psychological evaluations. For example, one psychologist diagnosed a parent with a condition that was no longer recognized! It was used in DSM-III (Diagnostic and Statistical Manual of Mental Disorders, 3rd edition), but removed from DSM-V, which was current at the time. Did he not know, or was he trying to fool the Court?

Virtually all psychologists, while testifying in court, failed to note that their predictions were not tested by long-term studies. They could easily be mistaken in individual cases.

Many psychologists stated hypotheses based on the evidence but failed to rule out other hypotheses which were just as likely. This is known in medicine and psychology as "differential diagnosis", and it is tedious. Some find it much easier to go along with what is expected.

Lawyers can never, but never, fail to challenge an expert; which means learning their field almost as well as you know your own.

I challenged one psychologist so fully that he later refused to take a case in which I represented a different client! But that was the exception; most clinical psychologists were cooperative.

Then there was a psychologist whom I'll call Dr. Raven, because he has a Baltimore accent. He diagnosed my client with "borderline personality disorder" (BPD) in a psych eval. When he took the stand, I pointed out that the mental illness bible, DSM-V, specifies that a BPD diagnosis requires a showing of at least 5 of 9 specified criteria. I asked which 5 my client had. He said he wasn't sure, and the Judge called a recess. During the recess, I saw Dr. Raven poring over books and notes in a conference room. When he got back on the stand, he had changed his diagnosis of the client.

I admit that I disliked Dr. Raven. Once my late wife and I had a foster kid who was lazy and unambitious. Dr. Raven was his clinician. He told us that we should "praise" the kid whenever he did anything. My late wife took this to heart and praised the kid for things like brushing his teeth. Needless to say, this only made him lazier. Dr. Raven may be an expert, but I don't know in what field.

I was not surprised, years later, to see that Dr. Raven was giving pep talks at management retreats. Maybe that was his niche - an educated Dale Carnegie, telling people what they wanted to hear.

CHAPTER 13: WHO DO YOU TRUST?

At this point I could calm down clients who were facing psych evals and generally tell them what to expect and how to behave. I could level the playing field somewhat. But the one sticking point remained: not knowing the MMPI-2 questions that could actually put you on a "bad" scale? Without that, I was just making educated guesses.

Of course I checked the internet for "actual MMPI questions", but they had been deleted. I continued using every search criterion I could think of.

Then a miracle happened. I discovered what seemed to be a book which had published the MMPI-2 questions before they had become a secret. Apparently, no one had thought to remove it from circulation.

Looking further, I found several libraries across the country where that book might be located. Then – mirabile dictu! – it appeared that the book was located at the UConn Library on the main campus in Storrs, CT. I drove to Storrs, found one of the few parking spaces for visitors, and trudged a few blocks to the Babbidge Library. I located the book in the card catalog, and then, actually trembling, found the book on the shelves. I opened it, really shaking by now, and there were the magic 567 questions of the MMPI-2.

Feeling like Aladdin who had found the Magic Lamp, I immediately went to the copiers and made two copies of the test, checking and double-checking that I had gotten each page with no smudges. Trying not to smile, I replaced the book on the shelf and left with my treasure trove.

At the office with this booty, now came the task of matching the questions, by number, to the scales as specified in the book. It was unbelievably tedious, taking dozens of hours. Then I had to draw conclusions. Without boring the reader, it came to this:

1. Be honest. Do not "make up" answers to allow for presumed shortfalls in prior answers. The test can catch this and mark you as "deceptive."

2. Admit to normal human foibles: you would rather win than lose; sometimes you gossip; etc.

3. NEVER admit to being depressed.

4. NEVER admit to violent thoughts. It's OK to be angry sometimes, but never violent.

5. NEVER admit that you don't want to be with people. It's OK to be by yourself sometimes, but anti-social tendencies are a no-no.

6. NEVER blame others for your problems (even if you think it's true sometimes).

7. NEVER admit to low self-esteem.

8. Stick to normal behavior: eating and drinking, but no binges.

9. If absolutely in doubt about an answer: check FALSE (or "Slightly True", depending on the test). You are less likely to be wrong.

I published this on a family defense lawyer blog. Many lawyers appreciated the guidance and asked for more details.

One of the MMPI-2 questions was "It is safer to trust nobody." You had to answer "Yes" or "No." Obviously, "No" was the preferred answer. If you answered "Yes", you would be flagged on such subscales as: needing of affection; cynicism; misanthropic beliefs; hostility; and even psychoticism (which turns out to mean "disconnected from reality"). Well, perhaps I can be cynical, but I am hardly disconnected from reality.

The answer to the riddle seems to be this:

If you read the question as "Do you think that everyone is a liar and a cheat who is out to get you?", then you should answer NO.

If you read the question as "Do you think that most people are honest in personal dealings, possibly less so in business dealings; but in any case don't have the same priorities as you do, and therefore you should personally verify matters that are quite important?", then you should answer YES.

Again, "Trust but verify."

It's all how you look at it. Personality tests are sometimes varied for different cultures, which have different norms than do most Americans. But even within America, people have different norms. The point is not to disparage personality tests, which are useful, but to illustrate their limits.

The MMPI-2 is no longer the test of choice. A psychologist friend kindly allowed me to take the PAI ("Personality Assessment Inventory") test in his office, which is a newer version of an objective psych test. It turns out that all psych tests are derivative of the MMPI-2, and my general advice still holds.

My advice also holds if you are taking a personality test for employment purposes; assuming you want a job in a firm that gives such tests.

Just for completeness, concerning the ink-blot test:

1. Look at each blot for 10-15 seconds before answering. Don't rush.

2. Don't move the paper around different ways.

3. NEVER say "This is…." Too bold. Instead say "This looks like…."

4. NEVER give violent or sexually themed answers.

5. Safe answers: PEOPLE TOGETHER; BIRDS; ANIMALS; LANDSCAPES.

6. Your answers should be one or two sentences, without explanations.

7. If the evaluator tries to bait you with "Are you sure…?" or "Don't you think…?", these are traps to see if you are too malleable. Stick to your guns.

I once met a CPS defense lawyer who turned out to be Rorschach's granddaughter. I avoided niggling her about the test.

The bottom line is this. It is staggering to contemplate how many parents have lost their kids, temporarily or permanently, because they were not prepared for a psychological evaluation. Simply mind-boggling. Whether or not this practice should be outlawed in CPS hearings is something I must leave to another day. But lawyers absolutely must help to level the playing field.

CHAPTER 14: ARE WE SOCIAL WORKERS OR GODS?

All states have what are known as "emergency removal" procedures, or ER. The acronyms vary by State (OTC, or Order of Temporary Custody, in Connecticut), but the idea is the same. If the investigating social worker finds that the kids are in "imminent danger", they can remove them for some period (typically 72 or 96 hours) upon approval of their management. At the end of that period, the kids must either be returned to the parent(s), or a court petition filed. Then a Judge, hearing evidence from both sides, will decide.

The procedure is similar to a restraining order. Typically, a woman, on her own affidavit (sworn statement), gets a temporary restraining order against her husband or boyfriend. Then shortly thereafter the man gets to come in and tell his side to the Judge.

We now consider the case of Stella and her husband Steve. The facts:

1. Stella and Steve had a child. They were getting a divorce.

2. The Family Court had awarded custody of the child to Stella.

3. The Family Court issued a no-contact protective order against Steve.

4. For some reason, on a complaint by Steve, CPS removed the child from Stella on a 4-day ER.

5. CPS then placed the child with Steve.

6. CPS then filed an abuse/neglect petition. That petition alleged no facts supporting imminent danger to the child.

7. The Juvenile Court scheduled a hearing on the abuse/neglect petition, but no hearing on the emergency removal, which Stella had hired me to contest.

8. When I asked why, CPS explained that the child had already been returned to a parent; albeit not the one it was taken from. Therefore, according to CPS, there was no ER, and no need for a hearing on that!!

The basis of CPS's decision was this: the State law [statute] said that if the child taken on an ER is "not returned home" within 4 days, then an ER hearing had to be held. But since the child was returned to a parent, they were actually "returned home."

The upshot was that Stella would have no opportunity to contest the removal, an obvious violation of her due process rights as a parent.

This was beyond the pale. Even a Judge has no power to order ER of a kid and then deny the parent an opportunity to be heard. But CPS social workers, who are not lawyers, let alone Judges, had acted as Family Court Judges whose actions were not even reviewable! It was unprecedented.

I wrote a blistering motion saying that this State statute was unconstitutional as to Stella. The statute obviously meant "not returned home to the parent from whom the child was taken." Everyone in the world understood it to mean that, but it simply wasn't so expressed. Such things are common in the law.

I also noted that if Steve had thought the child was in imminent danger, he could have filed an emergency motion in Family Court, and a Judge would hear it However, more and more, parents are discovering that it is easier (and cheaper) to have CPS do their work for them

My motion asked that CPS be ordered to return the child to Stella immediately. In the alternative, CPS could file an ER petition and allege actual facts in support of imminent danger, which we would challenge in Court. (I listed the child's good care by Stella in the motion).

At that time, in that Juvenile Court, the Court Clerk was a lawyer who had the habit of reading a lot of the filings that came in. He read my motion, knew something was wrong, and took it straight to the Judge. (Yes, that was not strictly proper, but things are less formal in Juvenile Court).

The Judge absolutely hit the roof, called in the CPS lawyer (who had a permanent office at the Court), and gave him what-for. The lawyer called the CPS manager, and the child was immediately returned to Stella. CPS didn't even bother to allege imminent danger.

Of course the CPS lawyer knew nothing of CPS's actions in advance. But CPS has its own in-house lawyers. Why didn't the social worker check with those lawyers? Clearly, CPS despises lawyers who might hinder them, even when they are their own employees.

The next thing was to ask my legislator to file a bill that would change the emergency removal statute to say what it means. For that, I needed the support of the CPS Commissioner. Sadly, the Legislature is too frightened to act without her approval, lest they be accused of being "soft on child abuse."

In a face-to-face meeting, the Commissioner agreed that I was right but refused to support the bill. She claimed that this "would never happen again." I said fine, but what happens if the next Commissioner has a different opinion. I was left with a tut-tut, and that was that.

So much for courageous State Legislatures.

But at least the disaster was fixed. Yet CPS overreaching is never fixed.

Imagine: CPS social workers, who are not lawyers, and certainly not Judges, simply "determined" that the kid should be with the father, despite what a Family Court Judge had ruled. They further argued that the mother should have no opportunity to contest the emergency removal. This is worse than Russia or North Korea.

~~~

CPS once tried to extend its administrative powers in a way that would surprise even Socialists. This was not a case that I handled.

A Connecticut state statute makes it crystal-clear that reasonable parental physical discipline of a child is not considered criminal assault. One day in 1999, an ex-husband complained to the police that his ex-wife had spanked their child. (Divorce is the case that never ends). The police investigated and found nothing. The ex then complained to CPS, which believes (not unreasonably) that all corporal punishment of children is wrong. Despite the state law, the mother was substantiated for child abuse. Under the rules of the time, she was automatically placed on the Child Abuse Registry for life. (Those automatic rules are thankfully no longer in place).

The mother appealed to the Superior Court, which dismissed her appeal. She then appealed to the Appellate Court, which thankfully reversed the trial court and took her off the Registry. [For those interested: Lovan C., 86 CA 290, 860 A.2d 1283 (Conn. 2004)]. And it took five years to resolve this bureaucratic overreaching.

The Appellate Court came to the rather obvious conclusion that if the State Legislature specifically allowed something, CPS could not penalize you for doing it.

It is a wonder that CPS did not appeal to the State Supreme Court. Probably they were afraid that word of their "We are God" attitude would for once reach the public ear.

I sometimes wonder if CPS has a special staff group that just sits in a room and dreams up new torments for parents.

Limited government is here for a reason. It is true that the Founders did not envision computers, airplanes, air conditioning, and nuclear weapons. But they did envision that greed and laziness are an everlasting part of human nature, and they sought to counteract it to the extent possible.

CPS does protect kids. But when it overreaches, it must be stopped. Its powers must be checked.

It is a personal gratification for me to rise and say "Your Honor" to a Judge. I wonder if Americans realize how lucky we are to have an independent judiciary.

CHAPTER 15: A PROMISE IS A PROMISE

When a kid has to be placed in a foster home, a relative is always preferred. CPS naturally investigates the relative's home to see if it is suitable. It also investigates the persons living in that home.

However, when the relative lives out of state, CPS cannot go directly to that state and investigate. Instead, the local CPS (called the "home state") asks the CPS in the relative's state (called the "receiving state") to investigate the relative. This process is known as an "interstate compact", or IC. CPS in the home state will rely on the results from the receiving state.

Two kids were properly taken from their mother in Connecticut and placed in a foster home in another town. Then the mother's sister, Rebecca, called CPS and let them know that she would gladly take the kids. Rebecca lived in Upstate New York, had a husband, four kids, and a nice home. The kids were also bonded to her. It seemed like a no-brainer.

Connecticut CPS notified Rebecca that an IC. would have to be completed. However, Connecticut never initiated the paperwork to do so!

The reason is that Connecticut CPS had promised the current foster parents that they would get to adopt the kids! They had no right to do this, but they did it anyway. They did it for exactly one reason: it was the quickest way to get the matter cleared up and off their desk. IC's take paperwork and time; why bother when you can just stonewall the aunt?

Rebecca, a bright person, realized she was getting the runaround and called our office.

First, we got Rebecca to formally intervene in the Juvenile Court case. This is a simple procedure, allowing one to participate in an otherwise closed proceeding. But lay persons are generally not aware of it, and CPS never tells them about it.

Second, we pressured CPS to start the IC. paperwork. They knew we had the threat of a court motion to back it up.

Third, we pressured the New York authorities to move on the matter. Receiving states aren't always crazy about IC's either.

This simple-sounding investigation turned out to be incredibly tedious. But finally, one full year after the kids had been removed, Rebecca was licensed by New York State for foster care.

Four months later, the Connecticut Judge ordered the kids transferred to Rebecca in New York, against CPS's recommendation.

Part of the Judge's decision read as follows:

"The timetable related to the handling of [Rebecca's] request to be a placement resource for these children is egregious.

"[State law specifies that] there shall be a rebuttable presumption that an award of legal guardianship...by any relative who is licensed as a foster parent...shall be in the best interests of the [children].... [if] such relative is a suitable and worthy person...

"[W]here the legislature has spoken, the court [has no other] option."

In other words, the Judge, after finding that Rebecca was a suitable and worthy person, lectured CPS on the law, which it already knew but had chosen to ignore.

The Judge did not order sanctions against CPS; a pity. But he knew how common this is. And it is unlikely that the actual social worker was at fault; social workers do what their supervisors tell them to do.

Another victory for an independent judiciary. And another family reunited.

And another case of bureaucratic laziness, unprofessionalism, irresponsibility and lying gone unpunished.

CHAPTER 16: ASSORTED VIGNETTES

Jaspar become romantically involved with a gal, and they had a child before they were ready. There was immaturity and domestic violence. The gal had serious mental health issues. CPS properly removed the child.

Then Jasper got his act together. He and his mother petitioned to get the kid back. CPS filed a status report that was wholly inaccurate. Jasper's court-appointed lawyer was refusing to help him. That's when Jasper, with his mother's help, hired me.

The status report said, among other things:

Jasper was an uncaring father. We got the pediatrician to refute that.

Jaspar had a felony record. We found that it was only misdemeanors.

Jaspar was unemployed. That proved to be simply untrue.

Jasper's mother was mentally unstable. We got a clinician and a psychiatrist to refute this.

Lie after lie. One wonders who prepared this status report. But we did tell CPS and provided our evidence.

Also, CPS had not been giving Jaspar enough visits. A few pointed e-mails changed that. Jaspar had also been having trouble connecting with his CPS-appointed service providers, who weren't returning his calls (probably due to overwork and low pay). Some pressure fixed that also.

ASIDE. Pressure on CPS works when CPS knows that you are not afraid to file a court motion and ask that they be held in contempt. If you're nothing but a talker, like Atty. Stentor, you are invisible.

Now came the pretrial conference. It was a disaster. CPS claimed to have none of the evidence that we had provided! It turned out that one of its in-house lawyers had "buried" my letters and then claimed that they had not. You cannot make this stuff up.

CPS, for once, showed embarrassment. A new, top-flight social worker was assigned. A different CPS lawyer got on board. Within five months, Jasper's son was reunited with Jasper and Jasper's mother. Still too long, but how long would it have taken if CPS had gotten away with its shenanigans?

Your tax dollars at work.

~~~

At the age of three, Luther tried to have sex with his mother. The psychologists tell us that such behavior is never inborn; it must be learned from prior abuse. Needless to say, no one owned up to the abuse, and Luther was removed. I was his court-appointed lawyer.

Luther bounced around from one home to another, but they were simply not equipped to help him. Finally, an excellent facility was located in Massachusetts, the next state north. I pushed CPS to place him there, and no one objected. But the cost was high, and CPS dragged its feet.

I kept on it, and finally CPS agreed. A social worker called and said that everything would be all set in two weeks. I was ecstatic.

Three weeks went by, and no call. I called, and the worker said, "It's all done." "Great!", I replied, "Where is he and who do I communicate with?"

"Oh no," the worker corrected. "I mean that I have completed my paperwork. It's now on someone else's desk." When that part would be done, they could not say.

Only in a bureaucratic world, where people are pigeonholed and trained to act like robots, could "It's done" mean "It's not done, but I am."

I wrote to the CPS Commissioner and threatened to go to the Governor and the newspapers. Two weeks later, Luther was placed in the Massachusetts facility. Whether that would have happened anyway, who knows?

Lord be praised, Luther got good treatment and eventually returned home. I found out that he became a healthy young adult; well into middle-aged by now.

The Army is famous for popularizing the expression "It's not my job." Still, I never heard any excuse in the Army as bad as this one.

~~~

Nathan and his wife had two sons. Let's just say that they couldn't get along, and guardianship was transferred to an aunt. Nathan had also been arrested for domestic violence, and violation of a probation order.

But Nathan was getting his life back together. Always gainfully employed, he had stopped drinking and was active in counseling. He finally divorced his wife and was well on the road to recovery.

However, Nathan told me that he was facing 15 months in jail for VOP (violation of probation). His criminal lawyer was proud that he had gotten such a good deal for him. But I wondered: jail would end his employment and his visits with the boys and could wreck his chances at reunification.

I got a release and spoke to the criminal lawyer. He had been unaware of the Juvenile case (clients seldom tell you everything). I tried to explain, but he insisted it didn't matter and would not listen.

Later on I discovered the reason: the lawyer was plea-bargaining Nathan's life away, because he was afraid that Nathan did not have any more money beyond the initial retainer! He wanted to get the case over with. Even the Probation Officer said that Nathan had rehabilitated and did not deserve jail; but the lawyer had not even spoken to him.

Nothing to do but tell Nathan that I should also represent him in criminal court. I replaced Perry Mason, talked to witnesses and the State's Attorney, and wrote a pretrial brief. As a result, Nathan pled to a misdemeanor and got probation only. His boys were shortly thereafter placed with him, not the ex-wife.

Nothing mysterious here. Just doing the job.

~~~

Does luck ever matter? See for yourself.

Ricardo and Marguerite were successful American professionals. They were born and raised in a country that has, shall we say, less liberal ideas about how to raise children. When the kids got older and started to rebel, the parents responded sternly. The kids, having learned from their peers, complained to their teachers, who as mandated reporters called CPS.

CPS visited the home. The parents let them in, knowing nothing about a child protection system. They became incredulous and hostile when told that the methods of discipline that they had learned all their lives were now being questioned by the State. The meeting turned hostile, and an unfortunate tone was set. CPS responded by filing abuse/neglect petitions and hauling them into Juvenile Court.

Ricardo simply could not conceal his disdain for CPS, which only made defending him harder.

We settled on PS with reasonable specific steps. The kids got lucky and were assigned one of the better lawyers. They visited the kids, studied the reports, and concluded that CPS intervention at this point was doing more harm than good.

Finally the time came for PS to end. But a particularly vindictive social worker, with the CPS lawyer's help, filed a motion to extend it. Ricardo was apoplectic.

We got to court on the motion to extend.

The regular Judge was out that day. Instead, we got a Judge, an American-born Caucasian, who had served in the military and had been stationed in Ricardo and Marguerite's country of origin. He knew the culture and respected it. He realized that this was not a matter of abuse or neglect, but just a matter of American culture shock. PS ended that day, and CPS was out of the picture.

A few years later, the oldest "abused" child was doing well in college.

~~

There are several lawyers in the U.S. who represent the Saudi Arabian government. One of them, in New York City, was hired to represent exchange students studying in the Northeast.

When one of those students in Connecticut got a visit from CPS, the NYC lawyer found me and asked if I would represent the couple. The lawyer would pay the freight (with Saudi money).

No need to detail the case, as it was just more American culture shock. The husband was an actuarial student. The wife was adorned head-to-toe in veils and robes; one could only see her eyes. The boy, 3 years old, was adorable. I once brought him a toy airplane, and he had a grand time with it.

It was over soon enough. At the end I said to the husband: "I know that the U.S. and the Saudi's have different cultures. I prefer my own, and I understand that you prefer your own. But when I look at America and see pornography even on TV and magazine ads and billboards, and drinking and drugs out of control, I can begin to understand why you do as you do."

No, I am not favoring the curtailing of women's rights. I am only saying that there are many ways to look at cultural differences.

CHAPTER 17: CPS SURVIVAL GUIDE

Believing that this essay should contain some useful information, I am including a chapter on how to best avoid CPS in the first place. I will also discusshow to deal with them if they do show up.

Recall that CPS gets involved when it gets a referral, that is, a call from someone that there may be a problem. Calls can be from mandated reporters, such as teachers, social workers, or doctors; or from ordinary citizens, such as your neighbors or your own children; or from the police in the course of an investigation.

There is no guaranteed way to avoid a referral. However, if you follow these guidelines, you should minimize your chances of getting a knock on the door.

And be clear: your social standing and reputation in the community do not matter. ANYONE can be referred.

REFERRAL SOURCE: THE POLICE

Police normally get involved when there is a domestic violence (DV) call, which could be physical violence or a loud argument.

You should recognize that all couples have disagreements. Keep yours private and quiet. If that is not possible, seek help from a therapist. And listen to that therapist: there are few if any absolute rights or wrongs in DV situations.

Professional help can be costly. However, many towns have local agencies that can help, although there may be a waiting list. You can keep your temper by realizing the consequences of a visit from CPS.

DV must be nipped in the bud. If you are a serious victim, it is absolutely true that you will have to choose between your partner and your kids.

Please: keep your disputes private and quiet. Kids learn by example. You don't want them to see excessive squabbling and yelling. They may adopt it when they get older.

REFERRAL SOURCE: SCHOOLS

There is no question but that schools are the major source of CPS referrals. School personnel are mandated reporters. They are scared to death of not reporting anything, since it might come back to haunt them and ruin their careers. Teachers are, in effect, unpaid CPS agents.

It is absolutely essential to keep on good terms with your kids' teachers and any school social workers. This is black and white; true without exception.

If your kid has a bruise, don't assume that the teacher will treat it as just another incident of childhood. Call the school and send a written note, explaining exactly what happened to cause the bruise, and when.

Encourage your kid to talk to you if they have any problem. Kids have a tendency to "just talk" to their teacher. But what the kid sees as no big deal, the teacher may see as a potential referral. In other words, don't let the teacher become a substitute parent. You are the problem solver. If this sounds like a McCarthyite society: it is.

If your kid is being bullied, see the next chapter, "Bully for You." The school administration is positively useless in this sort of thing, and it can mean real trouble.

As a side note: CPS absolutely detests home schooling. The reason is that with home-schooled kids, CPS loses its major source of referrals. If CPS ever badgers you about home-schooling your kids, do not argue – call a lawyer who specializes in home schooling defense immediately. Don't be bullied by CPS into giving up your rights.

If you do have a problem with a teacher or other school staff, do your best to solve it locally. Call a lawyer if necessary. But again: don't get on the teacher's bad side.

REFERRAL SOURCE: NEIGHBORS

Keep on good terms with your neighbors.

Keep the noise down and the yard clean. If a dispute gets heated, it may be best to call a lawyer before it escalates further.

Neighbors are right on top of you and can be nosy. This is one reason why suburban homes tend to get fewer referrals than urban apartments; but they still happen.

REFERRAL SOURCE: BIRTHING HOSPITALS

The worst thing that can happen is if the baby is born addicted. Obviously, you should avoid alcohol and illegal substances during pregnancy. This can result in fetal alcohol syndrome (FAS), which is incurable at present and may lead to lifelong problems for the child. FAS is a totally avoidable type of child abuse. If you have a problem, seek professional help before getting pregnant.

Even if the baby is not born addicted, your blood or urine may show the presence of illegal substances. Laws vary from state to state; but it remains best to avoid illegal substances altogether. States may declare marijuana legal to get tax revenue, but that doesn't make it good. And you thought the State was there to protect your safety!

REFERRAL SOURCE: HOSPITAL EMERGENCY ROOMS

Hospital ER's often make referrals with the speed of lightning. If at all possible, take the kid to your regular pediatrician.

If that is not possible, and you must go to the ER, be prepared in advance with your explanation of the injury, including time and place and persons present, with as much specificity as possible. Explain it calmly and rationally and do not appear nervous or talk too fast.

If the hospital does call CPS, contact a CPS defense lawyer before you speak to them. Trust me: it makes no difference if you are totally innocent. I simply don't have time for medical horror stories, but they are not uncommon. Suffice it to say that one couple I represented had their kid taken away for supposed physical abuse. It turned out that he had brittle bone disease, but no physician would test for it until we contacted our own expert. True medical laziness and irresponsibility; just take the easy way out.

There is a new medical sub-specialty called "child abuse pediatricians." As an expert lawyer friend once told me candidly, most of them are frustrated surgeons who couldn't make the grade. They have developed a specialty of making CPS referrals. Don't argue with them; that only makes it worse. Get your own orthopedist, radiologist, neurologist, or whatever other specialists you need.

Again: do not argue with doctors.

NOTE: Readers interested in knowing more about CPS medical disasters are referred to "They Took the Kids Last Night", by Atty. Diane L. Redleaf.

REFERRAL SOURCE: PHYSICIANS

You must get along with your pediatrician or change them immediately. No waiting.

The worst case is when you disregard the pediatrician's recommendation on anything, such as vaccinations, feeding routines, etc. Disregarding doctors is almost certain to lead to a referral. Get someone else.

One thing you often hear is that the child is not gaining weight fast enough. In the lingo, this is called "failure to thrive." If you hear that, take it seriously, and see a specialist if the problem persists.

Also, if other doctors are involved with your kid, you have to personally follow-through and ensure that the doctors are communicating with one another. Real life is not like the TV drama House. Doctors are particularly notorious for communication problems, often relying on their staff who may or may not see the problem. Be proactive and check it out yourself. You won't be sorry.

I once wrote a long letter to the Hartford County Medical Society, offering suggestions for avoiding medical communication problems. Of course, it got no answer.

REFERRAL SOURCE: IN-LAWS

As the old saying goes, if you wouldn't like to be married to the mother or father in 20 years, then don't marry the daughter or son.

Newspaper advice columns are full of: they aren't raising my grandchild properly; they keep interfering with my parenting; etc. I certainly can't solve this centuries-old problem, but I advise you to take it seriously. If the in-laws give any indication that they will call CPS, then you call a CPS defense lawyer before it's too late.

REFERRAL SOURCE: YOUR OWN KIDS

In Orwell's classic book 1984, a political prisoner said that he was proud of his own son for turning him in for denouncing Big Brother. "I must have raised him right." In real life, it is nothing to be proud of.

As mentioned earlier, kids learn the system. At least 95% of referrals that kids make on their own parents are bogus.

One suggestion is to avoid physical discipline unless 100% necessary. It seldom works anyway. Never leave marks on kids. Use time-outs or other privilege losses. If the kid has serious problems, you must see a qualified therapist right away. These problems seldom go away on their own. At least you will have covered yourself, and it may even do some good.

Out-of-control kids are simply your cross to bear. Handle it, and don't get trapped yourself. Again: behavioral problems seldom go away on their own; although it occasionally happens with maturity. But don't wait for it. Therapists can help.

In a split custody situation, never use the kid as a pawn to carry on against the other spouse. Not only does this not work, but it often leads to referrals by the other spouse. Save your disputes for the lawyer.

No matter what you do or don't do, your kid can "just talk" to a friend or a teacher, and CPS will show up at the door. You can only try your best. Again, urge your kids to talk to you if they have a problem.

~~~

And if CPS does show up at your door, or calls you in to their office, you have three choices:

1. Tell them to go to Hell;

2. Open up and smile and answer everything, on the grounds that you catch more flies with honey than with vinegar;

3. Follow the "CPS Survival Guide" appearing below.

The first option is not recommended. You do not have to let them in without a warrant. But openly challenging them will invite further action, and they will almost always get to you somehow. It will be nasty. Throughout the life of the case, your non-cooperation will be noted. Therefore, getting angry at CPS, while understandable, is not the way to go.

As to the second option, if it worked, there would be no jobs for CPS defense lawyers. An explanation is in order.

Suppose the police are investigating a bank robbery. They have 10 persons of interest, and you are one of them. If you are innocent and present an alibi, everyone will be happy. You, because you're off the hook; and the police, because they have one less suspect to investigate.

If CPS is investigating child abuse or neglect, they normally will not look to any other suspects but the parents. There is no alibi that will get rid of them; they will keep digging. The more you answer, the more they will ask. The more releases you sign, the more they will investigate and ask you to sign yet more releases, and go for treatment and services. It seldom ends. There is no presumption of innocence and no jury trial.

As to the third option, I used to have a "CPS Wallet Card" that I offered free to anyone.

An updated version will now be presented. So, if you do get a CPS referral, and a CPS investigator comes to the door or summons you to their office, here's what you say:

CPS SURVIVAL GUIDE

1. I will allow you to see my kids at the door for a "well-child-check", so you can see that they appear OK.

2. I believe in child protection and will cooperate with you fully, but through my lawyer. Please provide me with your business card.

3. As soon as I retain a lawyer, we will set up a meeting at the house where the lawyer will be present. Please do not threaten to take the kids unless I allow you in right now, as you do not have that authority.

4. I will sign documents only after my lawyer reviews them. Please do not tell me that it is routine, or standard, or just an office form, or anything to that effect.

5. After I have conferred with my lawyer, you may speak to my children without my being present, as long as the lawyer is present.

It goes without saying that you should not discuss the case with anyone else. I know this is a very human tendency, but please resist it. No good will come of it, but a lot of harm can result if your friend gives you "advice."

And please avoid internet advice, except from qualified CPS defense lawyers. From personal observation, I know that much of it is either nonsense or might not apply to your jurisdiction. Don't try to out-lawyer your lawyer.

With CPS, you have to be proactive, but rational.

For suggestions on finding a lawyer, see the chapter on "Getting Legal Help."

Note: Today even little kids know their Miranda rights. But very few parents are aware of their rights when dealing with CPS. One reason is that you seldom see CPS cases on TV or in the newspapers.

CHAPTER 18: BULLY FOR YOU

Bullying is one of the problems of life that seem to happen over and over.

Virtually all bullies are insecure. This explains why kids engage in it so much. But there are plenty of adult bullies, ranging from the simple work harasser to Hitler and Stalin. Almost all adult bullies are both insecure and cowardly.

If you realize that bullies are insecure, and generally cowardly, you will understand how they find victims. They sight someone who also appears to be insecure and may be an easy mark. Then they try them out. If the bullying works, they keep it up (sincere apologies to my Christian friends, but turning the other cheek does not work). If you stand up to the bully, they usually back down. Even Hitler would have been stopped in his tracks if people had stood up to him early enough.

The intimidation of the victim makes the bully feel more secure. That is the motive for the behavior.

Early on at the insurance company, I had a guy try to bully me. I stood up to him and bitched him up and down, threatening to go to the President of the company if he did it again. It worked. For the next 18 years, I never heard a peep out of him.

Later on, as a lawyer, I was discussing that bully with a friend who still worked at the Company
. She told me, oh yes, he harassed people all the time, especially the women. When I asked why no one had ever spoken up or reported him, she gave me a blank look.

And thus do bullies succeed. I have often thought that victims, deep down, have a feeling that they are unworthy and deserve it. Hence, they don't complain. Do you fit the bill?

Which brings us to school bullying. This is often just a normal part of growing up. But what happens when it affects your kid's performance at school, and possibly their entire life?

Adults know that if other adults harass them, they can seek legal action; criminally or civilly. Even at work, it should be possible to complain to Human Resources – especially if you get your lawyer to write the letter. But when kids harass other kids at school, what do you do?

The first response of most parents is to complain verbally to the school. That is, without question, the worst thing you can do.

School administrators are in business to keep things tidy. They are not courts of justice. They will tell you whatever you want to hear, never in writing, and string you along. If you keep complaining, they will act as though you are the problem.

One reason for this is that if the school goes after the bully, their parents will likely raise hell. If the bully is a minority, the school may be in for a civil rights lawsuit. Also, administrators have better things to do than to adjudicate kid disputes, which normally results in outcomes that make everybody mad.

To protect themselves, most schools, backed by State laws, have procedures to write down all incidents of bullying reports. This leads many parents to believe that the school is responsible for "doing something" about the bullying. Surprise – it generally is not, and almost always is immune from lawsuits that say it didn't do enough (the government does protect its own). There are cases of successful lawsuits against schools, but those are rare and not something to bank on.

If you think that your kid is being bullied to the point where it affects their school or personal life, here are the suggested steps:

1. Hire a lawyer who is familiar with school law.

2. Have the lawyer meet with your kid and review the entire story in detail. All facts must be gathered, pro and con. It may be better if the parents are not present, but it depends. You want the kid to be absolutely truthful.

3. Assuming the lawyer determines that there is at least a reasonable probability of harmful bullying, have the lawyer write a letter to the School Principal with a copy to the Superintendent. That letter will also get to the Board of Ed and its lawyers in no time flat.

4. The letter must allege SPECIFIC FACTS and ASK FOR SPECIFIC REMEDIES.

5. NEVER, NEVER, NEVER discuss this matter yourself with school personnel verbally. Administrators are trained in how to schmooze people without leaving a written record. Do not succumb to this, no matter how tempting. ("Come on, Joe. We're old friends. et's settle this without lawyers."). Verbal assurances in school matters are the kiss of death.

6. If the school stonewalls you, the lawyer can take the appropriate action, depending upon your jurisdiction's rules. Remember: expect stonewalling. Let the lawyer handle it; the school hopes you lose your temper.

7. For some reason, adults are not aware that the criminal law also applies to children, although with less force. If your kid is being assaulted, have your lawyer write to the bully's parents, and threaten to go to the police AND to file a civil lawsuit. That will normally get the parents' attention. Warning: the cops don't like getting involved in this sort of thing, so make sure you can prove assault, and have your lawyer pester the police to act and issue a Juvenile Court summons if necessary.

8. If there is no assault, but only taunting behavior, have your lawyer investigate the possibility of a civil action for infliction of emotional distress against the bully (through their parents). No parent wants to go to court

Remember, do not take these serious steps unless your lawyer independently determines that you have a real case. If so, you cannot beg the school to act. You must give the school a chance, but not a way out.

After all, you don't want to teach your kid to act like an unworthy victim who deserves it.

But please: don't expect the school to help you.

For those hardy souls who think they don't need lawyers, consider the actual case of Daniel Scruggs. Daniel was a Meriden, Connecticut middle school student who had been relentlessly bullied for years, and one day he hanged himself. His mother claimed that she had tried to get help but was stonewalled by the authorities.

Naturally, after Daniel's suicide, there was an investigation. The result: the mother was arrested! The State charged that, bullying or not, her negligence was the main cause of Daniel's death. Despite having one of the best criminal lawyers in the State, she was convicted but mercifully spared jail time.

God be thanked, in August 2006, the Connecticut Supreme Court unanimously reversed the conviction and ordered an acquittal. The Court noted, among other things, that CPS had closed its file on Daniel's case. This led the mother to believe that the State itself believed that there was no threat to Daniel.

Please do not think "that was 2006; things are better today." They are not. The only change today is laws mandating more paperwork that the schools can and do use to bury their own inaction.

Mrs. Scruggs later filed a federal lawsuit against the school system. It was settled out of court. The government's attitude surely was: "Well, we did nothing wrong, but it was worth it to get rid of her."

I don't blame you if you think that all of this is hard to believe, and I must be exaggerating. After all, no one goes into education to get rich. Don't administrators really want to help kids?

They do, but their hands are tied. In 1980, President Jimmy Carter, to reward the teachers' unions for supporting him, created the Federal Department of Education (DOE). As you might imagine, DOE resulted in more laws, regulations, paperwork requirements, national standards, lessening of local control, and lawyers upon lawyers; all to ensure that kids had more "rights" and an "appropriate public education." In practice, such education means that the problem kids are catered to rather than the serious students. Schools have become high-class baby-sitters; just ask any relatives and friends who are teachers, when no one else is listening.

The administrators thus have two main jobs: to see that no waves are made; and to push paper. Imagine if the manager of a small business tried to do their job, but had dozens of sets of rules and scores of people looking over their shoulder every second.

It's not really the administrators' fault, any more than it's the social workers' fault. That's the system. More joys of big government.

NOTE: People often write to Ann Landers or other advice columnists about school bullying. The answer is always trite. I would write to the columnist and give her the real scoop. It was never published.

One day, a local TV investigative reporter did a feature on school bullying. I wrote to her. She called, said she was interested, and would call me back. She never did.

Apparently, no one takes school bullying seriously, no matter what they say. As Mrs. Scruggs found out.

Agree with everything in this chapter or not, the bottom line is unassailable: bullies look for victims. You can't stop them from trying, but you can stand up to them with whatever is necessary to stop it. Just don't expect others to do it for you.

Lesson to parents: raise your kids to take pride in their achievements; and that doesn't mean playing video games or doing their homework for them. They will be less likely to become victims.

For years, I had hoped that the Federal DOE would be abolished. There must be a God, for Trump was elected and is attempting to do that as I write. No one who defends DOE has ever suggested that its results be audited. Why not?

CHAPTER 19: GETTING LEGAL HELP

It can be easier said than done to get a qualified CPS defense lawyer.

If you are hauled into court, and can prove financial need, the court will appoint you a lawyer. I recommend that you try to find the means to retain a private lawyer if at all possible.

The court will not appoint you a lawyer for non-court actions, such as investigations or Registry placements. You will have to retain a private lawyer.

Therefore, you can get a private lawyer for CPS court or non-court cases. The trick is to find one.

One way to start is the internet. Let us suppose you live in Mayes County, Oklahoma. You look up "Oklahoma child protective services agency" and find that its acronym is DHS – Department of Human Services. Then you look up "DHS defense lawyers in Mayes County, OK" and get a list. The list will consist of other types of lawyers, and lawyers in other counties, so you have to be careful. Do the same for any other county. It's a starting point.

A common method is to ask a lawyer for a referral. But be careful. Here's a horror story.

Georgette needed a CPS lawyer, so she asked a top-flight criminal and appellate lawyer, one of the best in the state, for a referral. He had a friend whose firm did Juvenile Court work and referred her.

That firm's Juvenile Court work turned out to be juvenile delinquency cases, also heard in Juvenile Court. These are totally different from CPS cases. The poor lawyer assigned to Georgette would not admit that she was in over her head. It took Georgette several months to realize that she was being had.

Georgette called us. Her case was almost too far gone to fix. But we managed, with the help of a sympathetic Judge.

The moral: no one knows everything. Even the best make mistakes. Caveat emptor.

A less common method is to go to the Juvenile Court yourself and ask the Clerk, or the Sheriff, for a recommendation. They may or may not give you one. I know of one case where it worked well.

The critical item, once again, is to ask and be sure that the private lawyer actually does contested CPS cases in court. This is not a time for ordinary criminal, divorce, child support, or juvenile delinquency lawyers. Please, take my word for this.

The national group of CPS defense lawyers that I tried to start [Chapter 7] would have published a lawyers' web site for the benefit of parents. Sadly, it did not happen.

If you believe your lawyer is ineffective, quickly take steps to get another lawyer. Don't count on suing your lawyer for malpractice. It is unlikely to succeed and will not get your kids back any faster.

If you have a court-appointed lawyer, ask the Judge for another one. Be sure to have SPECIFIC, detailed examples of the alleged malfeasance.

If you have a privately retained lawyer, search the internet or ask knowledgeable people for a replacement recommendation.

CHAPTER 20: FOURTH AMENDMENT PROBLEMS

As mentioned in the Survival Guide, you do not have to let CPS into your home without a warrant. However, it is generally advisable to let them in if your lawyer is present.

Of course, the famous 4th Amendment protects you against unreasonable searches and seizures. But there are many exceptions to needing a warrant, notably in emergency situations. Lawyers call these "exigent circumstances."

Can CPS demand entry into your home without a warrant?

No, but they can try. In 2005, a former Connecticut CPS Commissioner actually asked the Connecticut Attorney General if CPS could go into private homes, without a warrant, and without consent, on CPS matters. Fortunately, the AG said No.

This Commissioner, who was not a lawyer, failed to understand the implications of what she was asking. She actually released her memo. CPS has buried it, but I have a copy.

Yes, there is no limit as to what CPS can dream up.

Warrantless searches of homes would lead to what I call NRI, or "no-referral investigations." It would effectively wipe out the 4th Amendment, as long as you assert "child protection" as your reason.

Does this remind anyone of a totalitarian state?

Can't happen here? Will you take that chance? Be careful who you elect to office.

In all fairness, CPS was more cooperative with the 6th Amendment.

The 6th Amendment was interpreted by the U.S. Supreme Court in the famous Miranda case. It said, among other things, that the police have to tell a person in custody that they can have a lawyer present when answering questions.

So I had a whimsical thought. Why not require social workers to tell parents that they can have a lawyer present when answering questions. It is not required, as CPS cases are not criminal cases, but it would be nice.

After all, most parents would rather spend 6 months in jail than lose their kids. Too many parents are intimidated by people with State badges. They often think they have to talk, and it comes back to haunt them.

To my utter amazement, the then Connecticut CPS Commissioner agreed. A state law was passed requiring social workers to advise parents, on the first visit, that they can have a lawyer present. [C.G.S. Sec. 17a-103d]. A victory! I called it the Mini-Miranda Law.

Sadly, there is no redress if the worker fails to notify the parent. Their statements can still be used against them. The State Legislature would not go that far.

I put this out on the blog and got calls from around the country. By now, a few other states also have their own Mini-Miranda Laws.

CHAPTER 21: LICENSE TO PARENT

Are you still not afraid of CPS? Agent 007 had a license to kill. But an old leftist idea that's been kicking around for years is that you need a license to parent. You can look up "Licensing of Parents" on the internet and find some interesting reading.

The argument goes like this. We license people for difficult and critical jobs. You can't just work as a physician, dentist, veterinarian, plumber, electrician, lawyer, CPA, etc., until you have demonstrated certain skills. Surely parenting children is as critical as taking care of dogs or toilets, so why not license parents?

Fine, but who would do the licensing, and using what criteria?

Suppose that Gov. Gavin Newsom, like John F. Kennedy, is able to leverage his good looks into becoming President. He may take the Congress along with him. If the social workers' unions had supported him, he might reward them by pushing through a law for the licensing of parents. After all, President Jimmy Carter, hardly a radical, rewarded the teachers' unions for supporting him by pushing through the creation the federal DOE [see Chapter 18].

Licensing of parents would be administered by the federal Department of Health and Human Services [HHS], which would set criteria for the states to follow. And would only child molesters and obvious psychopaths be excluded? Don't bet on it. Leftists would also be in charge of HHS.

And leftists believe in cancel culture. Look at what happened to Harry Potter author J.K. Rawling. Leftists tried to cancel her for complaining that "people who menstruate" should instead be called "women." The media has identified hundreds of other examples, from famous celebrities to ordinary teachers and businesspeople.

Recall that even I was threatened with being cancelled and assaulted just for saying publicly that CPS social workers, as a class, were not racists. [see Chapter 11]. I strongly disagree with leftists but have never even thought of cancelling them.

Why couldn't cancelling be applied to parents and prospective parents who also express "unacceptable" views? Wouldn't these views make them "questionable" as parents? HHS and social workers could think so.

Impossible? Suppose I had said, during the 2020 Presidential campaign, that a Biden victory would result in the FBI's going after parents who protested at school board meetings that their young kids were being taught transgenderism.

Impossible indeed.

Licensing of parents is admittedly far-fetched by today's standards. But not that long ago, so was gay marriage, girls encouraged or forced to strip in front of and play contact sports against boys, schools teaching transgenderism to elementary students, violent criminals being released on the streets with no bond, unvetted criminals and terrorists entering the country, and homeless people taking over San Francisco. Nothing is impossible by "progressive" standards.

They are your children. Do you want to take the chance?

We live in a slippery-slope society. Yesterday's outrage is tomorrow's standard.

Let's take a look at some of the politically incorrect ideas you might hold that could suggest you were an unfit parent.

CHAPTER 22: DANGER: YOU STRONGLY

BELIEVE IN LAW AND ORDER

I was not around in cave man times, but I am reasonably certain that there was some of what we would call today "criminal behavior." Some cave man must have stolen another cave man's meat or fish. Some cave women must have stolen another cave woman's child. There was certainly sexual assault. As cave people settled into clans, there must have been leaders, and some sort of justice system. We recognize that there will always be criminals, and the goal is to deter criminal behavior, and deal with it when it happens. That "dealing" can include punishment, and restitution when possible.

All societies dealt with crime, some more effectively than others. The rich and powerful always got away with more than the common people, but gradually even wealthy criminals were brought to justice. In the U.S., we have seen Governors and Senators, and almost a former President, put in jail. Sadly, we have not seen enough business executives put in jail, as they hide their corporate crimes amidst layers of bureaucracy.

I have never been a member of law enforcement and claim no special expertise in this area. However, I personally hate crime. And worse, I hate those who encourage it.

In early 2018, Dr. Larry Nasser was convicted of molesting teenage girls for many years. He was sentenced to life and then some. There were no calls for defunding medical schools or replacing MD's with LPN's and social workers. Some of the scum who knew about Nasser but looked the other way were also penalized; but, I am certain, not all of them. So some form of justice was done, however untimely and incomplete. I am left to wonder why the people who knew about Nasser's crimes remained silent; apparently, they thought that winning the Olympics was more important than human lives. This is but another example of educated, intelligent people corrupted by greed and laziness.

On May 25, 2020, a black man named George Floyd was murdered by a Minneapolis police officer. The cop immediately lost his job, was arrested, tried, convicted, and imprisoned. The cops who stood by and allowed the murder to happen received lesser sentences. The Minneapolis Police Department came under federal scrutiny. Justice was done to the extent possible.

Yet there were calls to defund the police, or severely restrict them, or get rid of "qualified immunity." It would take too long to explain this legal concept, but what it means in practice is that police officers, who have to make split-second decisions, get no legal protection therefrom. It discourages people from becoming police officers, lest they lose their freedom and fortune from one good faith but unfortunate action made in the heat of battle.

As a side effect of George Floyd, the government took no action against rioters and looters who burned businesses of innocent people and even attacked federal buildings. Two wrongs don't make a right. But it could hardly have surprised leftists when Trump supporters felt free to attack the Capitol on January 6.

While only the far left called for full defunding of the police, that included some members of the U.S. Congress! (Is calling for destruction of the U.S. military the next step?) Normal leftists were more restrained, calling for "controls" over the police that would effectively hamstring them. Is it any wonder that our cities, and some towns, are out of control?

Of course some police do commit crimes. So do doctors, lawyers, school principals, business executives, accountants, politicians, and others. We deal with them individually, as with George Floyd's killers. But we don't get rid of them as a class, or hamstring them to the detriment of tens of millions of law-abiding citizens.

I have yet to meet the honest, law-abiding, taxpaying minority citizen who wants violent criminals running around in his or her neighborhood.

But the Biden Administration did more than denigrate the police. It actually encouraged crime by opening the border to unvetted illegal aliens, some of whom were criminals, terrorists, or persons with diseases. The most ordinary citizen could not help but notice that if the government itself flouted the law, why couldn't regular people do so. And thus you had far-left District Attorneys releasing violent criminals (not petty thieves) on bond, and ignoring ICE detainers.

I have to say that when George Gascone was defeated as District "Attorney" of Los Angeles County, it was one of the happiest days of my life; almost like the day I got out of the Army. There is hope even for Southern California.

The whole of the war on police is actually a sub-species of DEI. The thought is that too many blacks were arrested and imprisoned. Therefore, instead of correcting that problem, simply define it away by giving a pass to criminals. It's similar to correcting the problem of incompetent white managers by hiring incompetent black managers. The whole thing is an obvious disservice, if not total disrespect, to honest minority persons.

Everyone notices that the media pays little attention to crime in minority areas. When is the last time you heard that Chicago is the murder capital of the country?

Only insecure kids would join gangs and harm their fellows. This suggests that we need fewer "community activists" and more responsible parenthood. Kids who grow up hearing about respect for law and order, honest work, education, and respect for themselves and others, will seldom become criminals.

We need not even get into the politicization of the U.S. Department of Justice, or its failure to seek any meaningful charges against the Biden family for corruption. Does anyone believe that Hunter Biden, who made millions with no discernible skills, did not parcel out some of that money? And everyone wondered why the DOJ went after people who said prayers in front of abortion clinics, while ignoring criminals who set fire to federal buildings. Everyone except the mainstream media that is.

It is beyond doubt that Biden opened up the border for the purpose of buying votes. No one seriously doubts that. A collateral "benefit" was to provide cheap labor for his corporate friends.

Of course, some say that "the border was broken." This shows a failure of what used to be called Liberal Arts education. The Liberal Arts teach you to think, read, speak, and write critically. Thus, if someone says, "The border is broken", you will immediately ask "What does that mean?" Very simple.

If it means "the laws are wrong", then you get Congress to fix the laws.

If it means "the laws are right, but enforcement is lacking", then you get the President to enforce the laws.

If it means "the laws and enforcement are good, but interpretation of the law is lacking for want to judges", then you get more judges appointed.

But under no condition does it mean "Disregard the law and fail to enforce it."

But once Biden (or his handlers) saw that open borders meant fentanyl and obscene profits for criminal cartels at the expense of American lives, why did he not stop it immediately? This will remain a mystery for me until the end of my life. Why would he actually encourage criminal behavior?

I cannot imagine a single person in America, Democrat or Republican or anything else, other than the organized criminal class, who is not happy at President Trump's attempt to close the border and go after criminal cartels as terrorists. I have had people tell me "All border crossers are not criminals." That is true; but again, beside the point. Certainly for those who have lost relatives and friends to fentanyl.

Suppose you don't support BLM rioting, or illegal immigration, or releasing violent criminals on bond. Suppose you believe that to vote, a person must show an ID, just as if they wanted to withdraw cash from a bank or board an airplane. Suppose you don't support DEI. A leftist social worker could say you are a hater. It would be one piece of evidence to show that you are unfit to parent.

CHAPTER 23: DANGER: YOU ARE NOT A FEMINIST

In former days, when I worked at the insurance company, my late wife used to suggest that I read the Mars/Venus book. The goal was for me to better understand the so-called war between the sexes. Most people by now have heard of the theory. Men are from Mars, and their major complaint is that women criticize them too much. Women are from Venus, and their major complaint is that men don't listen to them enough. I kept resisting with one excuse or another.

Then I got an invitation to speak at a DP Auditors' conference in San Antonio, Texas. The food was outstanding; the history dazzling, to the point where I was in tears (I grew up watching Davy Crockett at the Alamo); the Riverwalk unequalled; and the people were incredibly friendly. I shall return.

The flight back was long and would stop to change planes in St. Louis. (This was in the fun days of flying). At the San Antonio airport, I saw the Mars/Venus paperback in a store and thought, what the heck, why not? So I bought it and finished it before arriving back in Hartford.

As I was reading the book, the movie Encino Man kept coming to mind. This was a high school comedy in which two geeky teens find a cave person trapped in ice and bring him back to life. The cave person turns out to be – surprise - a teenaged boy! So they train him in the ways of the world and bring him to their high school, passing him off as a foreign exchange student.

You can guess the rest. This movie, while widely panned as dumb, gathered a teenie cult following.

So I thought: what if we actually found an adult cave man frozen in the ice, brought him back to life, and he turned out to be bright. We could educate him in world history, modern inventions, our language, etc. We might be able to learn from one another.

When he was sufficiently up to date, we would put him in a library and invite him to read books and ask questions of his mentor.

As it happened, our cave man read the Mars/Venus book and asked to discuss it with his mentor. The conversation might go something like this:

"I don't understand this book."

"What don't you understand?"

"Well, you show me your modern inventions, and the great things you have accomplished, and then you give me this new book 'explaining' the differences between the sexes. I don't get it."

"What don't you get?"

"Men and women have different ways of looking at things. We knew that in cave man times. Why do you think that the sexes developed separate rites, such as hunting parties and sewing bees, and more modern get-togethers? And yet you present this as a new ground-breaking discovery, and it turns into a best-seller, sparking audiotapes and videotapes and even themed cruise ships."

"Well, we are trying to solve the problem."

"Let me ask you this. The 'problem' has been going on for thousands of years. Some of the best minds have considered it. And yet it remains. What does that tell you?"

"What do you think?"

"That we don't really want to solve this non-existent problem."

And so it is. What "moderns" fail to understand is that there has always been and always will be a certain amount of tension between the sexes. People want that. The tension is what keeps the spark alive. That's why virtually unlimited pornography and TV sitcoms full of sex jokes eventually fall flat. They remove the mystery of sex and turn it into a commodity.

This attempt to "solve" the "problem" must perforce fail of its own weight. If a man says he is listening, the woman will say, "Perhaps, but you don't really understand." If the man proves that he does understand, the woman will say "Yes, but it's not enough. You have to experience it." If the man says that he is not a woman and therefore can't experience it, the woman will say "Well, that proves my point." And if the man says that the woman criticizes too much, she will respond, "No I don't." And her response is truthful; because, to her, what she says is only observation, not criticism.

A friend once told me that the only thing that saves most marriages is precisely the fact that men don't listen enough to women. If they did, the divorce and split-up rate would be even greater than it already is. As the French say, Viva la difference!

Americans, as a class, like to believe that every problem can be solved. A State Legislator friend once told me of an encounter he had with a visiting German legislator. "One of the things that makes you Americans so charming, and so frustrating," said the German, "is that you believe that there is a solution to every problem."

Every one, apparently, except the ones that really matter.

What emerges from all this is that America is truly the marketing capital of the world. In what other country could a book as idiotic as Mars/Venus become a bestseller? We can market anything if we put sex or violence into it.

I must admit that I have an unusual approach to gender discrimination in law firm hiring. I had some male employees, but I much prefer female employees. And it isn't because you can pay them less. In a small cash-strapped firm, you can pay only so much whether you have males, females, or hermaphrodites. No, the reason is that males in our society are socialized to believe that their worth as human beings depends upon their salary. I don't know why this is so, but it is. I have seen guys quit a job that they really liked for one not as good but that paid 5% more. Women, as a class, are not like this. They are far more loyal and understanding of the limits of the business.

Is this prejudice, a pre-judging? Not really, because I have hired men, and I don't make assumptions in advance. But I have seen this phenomenon often enough. When today I hear the phrase "toxic masculinity," I get quite a different idea than the P.C. crowd does.

Feminism can be taken to extremes. One day, the CBA (Connecticut Bar Association) called me to be a judge in a middle school mock trial. Of course I agreed.

The day came and it went very well. One girl, about 14, did seem exceptional, and I wanted to speak to her. However, I knew that if I approached her, I would be branded as a sex offender. So I went to one of the chaperones, a guy over 6 feet tall (I am 5-7) and asked if we could speak. He said sure, and the three of us stood in the middle of the room, in front of scores of people, while the girl and I talked for about 2 minutes.

Two days later I got a call from the female CBA staffer who had run the event. It seems that someone complained that I had "approached" a young girl. I told the staffer what happened, and she said she would check it out. She called the next day and said "Never mind. All is OK."

I said I wasn't sure it was OK. Who had complained under these facts? She would not answer, merely telling me to drop it.

I didn't. I wrote to the Middle School Principal, told her the story, and asked what she would do about the person who made this asinine complaint – to say nothing of acting in a totally anti-education manner.

A week later I got a letter from the school's lawyer. It didn't address my question but said that if I had any matters to discuss with the Principal that I should write to the lawyer instead. The Principal herself couldn't be bothered to show any responsibility. She preferred instead to spend the Education Department's scarce resources on an overpaid lawyer.

Talk about living in a McCarthyite society. Education, indeed.

There is currently a school of thought that says that due process should be curtailed or eliminated whenever a woman makes a complaint against a man. Her word must be taken as
absolutely true, like the Pope when speaking ex cathedra. Needless to say, I disagree.

Suppose you don't support every tenet of feminism. Or you believe that men should have due process rights when accused by women. A leftist social worker could say you are anti-woman and would be a poor parent for a girl. It would be one piece of evidence to prove that you are unfit to parent.

CHAPTER 24: DANGER: YOU DON'T WANT MEN PLAYING IN WOMEN'S SPORTS

Gender dysphoria is a real thing. It refers to one's discontent between their assigned gender at birth and their preferred gender. Persons who want to read further are referred to the Diagnostic and Statistical Manual of Mental Disorders, 5th Edition, fondly known in the trade as DSM-5.

As a CPS defense lawyer, working with families involved in the Juvenile Court, I once had a case with an upper-middle-class conservative family who had four boys. The oldest boy had gotten into some trouble, and I helped him and his parents work it out. But the interesting thing was the youngest boy. He was born with gender dysphoria and had always wanted to be and acted like a girl. Now four years old, everything about him except his genitals was feminine.

The family accepted it and treated him and dressed him as a girl. He was seen by gender dysphoria specialists (clinical psychologists and psychiatrists who specialized in this area). Interestingly, I had to remind the family to go to Probate Court and get his name legally changed to a feminine one. Clearly, his gender dysphoria was real. He was too young to have formed politically-correct thoughts or be influenced by the schools or the media.

So there is no doubt that gender dysphoria is real. This boy had it caught in time, and by puberty will be a fully functioning female, except for an inability to have children. Others discover gender dysphoria after puberty, the most famous recent case being Olympic athlete Bruce Jenner, who became Caitlin Jenner.

Psychological conditions, like general medical conditions, are normally handled between patient and doctor. But for some incredible reason, gender dysphoria has become a political football. We have instances of physically- and sexually mature males ("PSMM"), obviously post-puberty, wanting to play against females in contact sports and live in their dormitories. We have school nurses and gym coaches who think they understand this condition and who try to handle it without even informing the parents. We have young kids forced to listen to lectures on a subject they cannot possibly understand. We have quotas for transgender people in positions of power.

How did this happen? How did a recognized psychological condition turn into a public debate involving lay persons who cannot possibly be qualified to handle it?

I am told that there is a "transgender lobby." Again, and sadly in a democracy, the ones who scream the loudest get the most media attention. This lobby has caused the incredible spectacle of persons who call themselves "feminists" agreeing that PSMM should be allowed to compete against girls and women, including stripping in front of them in locker rooms, and get medals and scholarships that the women thought they had earned.

My old high school buddy is a strong lifelong Democrat who hates Trump. He has granddaughters. I know he does not want them to be forced to strip in front of boys, but he is too intimidated to say anything, at least publicly.

Transgenders, homosexuals, short people, homely people, and handicapped people, and others, deserve to be treated with respect. That does not mean that boys (specifically PSMM) are in fact girls for sports purposes. That does not mean that unqualified gym coaches should handle a kid who think he or she is "conflicted" on gender. I have the highest admiration for Caitlin Jenner, who made it clear that PSMM should not compete against biological women. I simply don't understand why it had to be made clear.

President Trump, of course, has done the country a favor by abolishing subservience to transgenderism. But more importantly, he has done a huge favor to Democrats who were unable to speak their minds for fear of incurring public odium.

Of course mistakes will be made, and some individual hard cases will occur. But common sense must be re-established in America. The lesson to be learned is that we cannot give in to mobs simply because they scream louder than we do.

Suppose you are against females being forced to strip in front of PSMM. Or you don't think PSMM should play in contact sports against women. Or you don't want transgender ideas taught to elementary school kids. A leftist social worker could say you are transphobic and would reject a transgender child. It would be one piece of evidence to prove that you are unfit to parent.

In fact, in some states, kids can already get "gender-affirming care" without their parents' knowledge or consent. "Progressives" will stop at nothing.

CHAPTER 25: DANGER: YOU DON'T SUPPORT THE HAMAS CAUSE

The history of anti-Semitism is too well-known for general discussion. But with all the discrimination in the world, it is surprising that this one has recently taken center-stage.

I believe I know the reason. I reject the idea that it is some inherent dislike of the Jews. I believe it is anti-Americanism disguised as anti-Semitism, so that its perpetrators will not look like traitors. ("We are not against America or Jews in general, just the Zionists."). But American support for Israel is surely the driving force.

This is not to say that the Palestinians don't have an argument. They claim that they were driven from their lands. You could say the same thing about the American Indians. You could say the same about the Romans driving out the Etruscans, or any of thousands of other examples throughout history. What's done is done.

Why do educators not teach that anti-Semitism, like racism, homophobia, misogyny, Islamophobia, and other prejudices, is wrong? Are they too intimidated by the students to speak up? Are they not familiar with the details of October 6?

Incidentally, some of the worst antisemitism on campuses occurs in California. What has Gavin Newsom done about it?

I will never understand how the U.S. evolved into a society where "Progressives" condone violence. I am against almost everything that AOC says. But it has never occurred to me to physically block her from moving, or firebomb her office, or follow her into the ladies' room and harass her (as happened to one Republican Congresswoman). I have never thought of silencing or cancelling her. Where did this come from?

Suppose you don't fully support the Hamas cause. Or you gave money to Israel. Or you don't believe that sincere students should be allowed to disrupt college campuses and classrooms. Or physically intimidate those who oppose them? A leftist social worker could say that you are not sympathetic to victims. You favor genocide. You would raise an uncaring and violent child. It would be one piece of evidence to prove that you are unfit to parent.

CHAPTER 26: DANGER: YOU DO NOT BELIEVE IN THE GREEN NEW DEAL

I am not a climate scientist, or any kind of scientist, and don't claim to be. As a layman, I normally believe what the experts tell me. I don't question doctors on medical practices, and I don't tell electricians how to do their jobs.

Of course everyone knows that experts can be wrong. At one time all experts believed that the earth was flat. In modern times, experts told us that covid did not come from a leak in a lab that we had partially funded. Experts also told us that we had to virtually shut down our entire economy to prevent the spread of covid. This doesn't necessarily make you cynical; just skeptical.

Former Vice President Albert Gore came up with the idea that humans were causing the planet to self-destruct. Steps had to be taken to prevent this calamity. These steps were known as the Green New Deal.

The only problem is that the idea was erroneous. Most climate change is caused by solar activity, not by carbon emissions. However, by now, so many people had gotten rich on the Green New Deal that the idea proved difficult or impossible to stop. Kids who had no idea took up the mantle. It gave them something else to protest instead of studying.

Please do one thing: go to the web site www.clintel.org. You will be disabused of the Green New Deal forever.

Why were "climate deniers" silenced? Where was the free speech crowd and the ACLU? Where were the professors? Where were the historians who could have told us that catastrophe theories have proliferated throughout history?

Why is an opinion shared by hundreds of reputable scientists something to be banned?

Suppose you don't fully support the Green New Deal. Or you drive a big car or have a gas-guzzling lawn mower. A leftist social worker could say you are against saving the planet, and thus a danger to everyone. It would be one piece of evidence to prove that you are unfit to parent.

~~~

And you have to wonder: what's next? Possibly plural marriage, with opponents denounced as "polygamophobic".

It is common knowledge that leftist governments want the kids to look to the State, not to their parents, for guidance. That's why home schooling is banned in many leftist countries. You are advised to check into what your own public schools are actually teaching the kids. And doubly advised to watch out for any talk about the licensing of parents.

I have been involved with CPS for some time. There is very little that I would put past them. Licensing parents, along with warrantless searches of homes ("exigent circumstances: we are protecting defenseless kids") is an old idea. Progressives would say that its time has come. Progressives also believe in cancelling people that they disagree with. Put the two together: your licensing can be based upon your political views. It's similar to the "social scores" assigned to your political views in China or North Korea.

Of course, licensing of parents would eviscerate the Troxel decision. It would turn this nation into a clone of Communist China.

To repeat: They are your children. Do you want to take the chance? Be careful who you elect to power.

CHAPTER 27: CONCLUDING THOUGHTS ON CPS

I have a great deal of respect for CPS. It does its best work when it helps parents who have substance abuse (S/A) problems and are not aware of how damaging this can be to their kids. There are many excellent programs that help parents. These include S/A screenings and support and counseling services. And psychologists do tell us that parents with S/A problems are more likely to raise kids who also have S/A problems.

There are many adults who have such severe psychological problems that they are simply unable to parent children. One particularly sad disorder is called "co-dependency", which means in practice that the woman is so dependent on a man that she puts the man ahead of her kids. Sometimes she even allows child molesters into her home.

Other psychological problems are too numerous to mention, although DSM-V is a good reference. Sadly, some parents physically and sexually abuse their kids. Simply put, some people are not cut out to be parents.

Let me be clear: there are many excellent government workers. One CPS social worker, Catherine, was particularly caring. In court I once said to the Judge, "If all social workers were like The Cat, I'd be out of a job.

I once needed advice on starting my law business and made an appointment with the State Tax Dept. The staffer not only answered my questions, but pointed out many traps that I should avoid. He was like a paid personal advisor. I wrote a commendation letter. His supervisor replied that he was indeed the best, and they got such letters all the time. So it can be done. I only hope that he did not get "Peter-Principled" and promoted to a paper-pushing job.

Another time, I represented a grandfather who was trying to get custody of his grandkids who had been correctly taken from his druggie daughter. It seemed like a no-brainer, but CPS was adamantly opposed: the grandfather had had a misdemeanor conviction 20 years earlier. I convinced the CPS lawyer how ludicrous that was, and she arranged for the kids to go to the grandfather, CPS notwithstanding. I don't know how she did it, but she did. And of course I couldn't write a commendation letter. It might have destroyed a great career.

You sometimes wonder if there's a Gresham's Law of Business: bad people drive out good. Thankfully, not always.

I believe that it is better to have a CPS than not to have one. Thus, I reject the opinion of some who believe that CPS should be defunded, as they also believe that the police should be defunded. You can't solve a problem by creating anarchy.

And obviously, I vehemently disagree with those who believe that CPS is "racist." I know many of these folks, and I honestly believe that they have been co-opted by the Progressive Left. There is simply no evidence that I have seen to suggest that social workers "go after" minorities. In fact, quite the opposite.

One of my lawyer friends in New York has told me, "Michael, you are entitled to your opinions but not to your facts. Just stop being stubborn and look at the statistics that show...."

This argument is misplaced. As an example, the latest statistics show that blacks make up approximately 13% of the U.S. population but account for approximately 26% of the arrests. You can look at this fact and say that it proves that the police and DA's are racist. Or you can look at this fact and say that it proves that it is easier to arrest people for blue-collar crime than for white-collar crime.

Which view is correct? Well, name for me the social workers who are racists.

Progressives decline to do this but merely use the catch phrase "systemic racism." This is an undefined Alice-in-Wonderland term that means anything you want it to mean. Therefore, it means nothing. As Orwell pointed out decades ago.

I don't buy it. In fact, I think the reason for the CPS race-baiting is that it gives lazy lawyers an excuse to not do their jobs properly for their clients.

ASIDE. If anyone wants to play the race card on me personally: I have three black great-grandkids. As a CPS defense lawyer, I have helped more minorities than Al Sharpton and Jesse Jackson put together.

And just look again at Matthew Tirado's sad case [Chapter 11].

The problem, of course, is that CPS is a large government agency. The larger any organization, whether governmental or private, the harder it is to control, and the more chance there is for individual managers to build empires. Also, unions and workplace customs make it difficult to fire incompetent workers and managers. And even good people can succumb to irresponsibility and lack of integrity, when they are shielded by large organizations in which they want to please their supervisors.

All of which is to note the obvious: CPS can overreach. Paradoxically, it can also fall down on the job.

Overreaching and failures have led to many unjust outcomes. Some of these are illustrated here; others can be found elsewhere.

But that's not the end of it. It can get worse if licensing of parents, the old leftist dream, becomes a reality. Then not just your actions but your opinions could and would be held against you.

To repeat: they are your kids. Do you want to take that chance? Be careful who you elect to office.

And it would be nice if more CPS defense lawyers took their jobs more seriously. Their goal should be to reunite families when at all possible, and no reasonable effort should be spared to reach that goal.

It is noteworthy that law schools almost never teach CPS defense. When they do teach CPS, it is from the State's viewpoint. You don't normally see externships in CPS defense firms.

On one occasion, I had to rescue Yale Law School clinic students who tried to help a woman facing a DCF substantiation. They had no idea what they were doing. Their professor and their adjunct lawyer were no help. Afterwards, I asked the Professor if I could lecture to the class for one hour on CPS. He said he couldn't allow that. But he would have coffee with me if I came to New Haven.

Yet Yale has no problem holding protests against Donald Trump.

Why do law schools think they are adjuncts of the corporate state?

I have attempted to explain what CPS is and how it operates.

I have offered suggestions for avoiding CPS referrals.

I have offered suggestions for what to do if you are investigated. Be careful: your lawyer must have CPS defense experience.

I have also warned citizens of future dangers, such as evisceration of the 4th Amendment and the licensing of parents.

But please: Don't be scared; just be alert.

Thank you for your time.

I will be glad to answer reasonable questions and comments. Please e-mail me at:

attymikea@agranofflaw.com

However, please do not ask me to give legal advice on your specific CPS case. I am not your lawyer and could only refer you to a qualified CPS defense lawyer.

~~~

APPENDIX: MY PERSONAL RUN-IN WITH EQUITY

MORE DIVERSE THAN THOU

When I got my law degree from UConn, these were my credentials:

1. Second in my Evening Division class of 74 students.

2. GPA of 3.6, good enough for magna cum laude.

3. A publishable law review article that was subsequently published.

4. No criminal record.

5. Honorable Discharge, which is more than can be said for some Presidents.

6. Reasonably presentable and well-spoken.

7. Good recommendations from several professors.

8. Actual business employment which included the publication of several technical and administrative articles in national computer trade journals and speaking engagements at several national computer security conferences.

These were my job search results:

1. 42 job applications.

2. Zero acceptances.

What I failed to mention in my credentials was this: I was 46 years old when I graduated law school.

Recruiting started in the final year, that being September,1987. My initial first interview was with Robinson and Cole (R&C), one of Hartford's premier law firms.

I will never forget it. The interviewer, a senior associate, was wildly enthusiastic. "I have never seen a resumé as good as this," he said, several times. He went so far as to name the senior partner that I would be working with at R&C, one Atty. Donald Lee Rome (since deceased). Needless to say, I left with a euphoric feeling.

That euphoria faded as the expected second interview never came. It faded further, as I was not getting many other first interviews, even though friends with lesser grades were getting them left and right.

Some of the interviews that I did get were interesting:

1. One had a female interviewer in her late 20's. The second I walked into the room, she glared at me and frowned. The interview was openly hostile, and of course no second interview resulted.

> I wonder what UConn's reaction would have been if a black applicant had said that a white lawyer glared at him and had been hostile from the beginning.

2. Another, held at the firm itself, featured a very good interview with an associate. We got along well, and he said that he wanted the senior partner to meet me. In came a man in his 60's, Jewish like myself. He frowned at me, picked up my resumé, frowned again, looked at me, and said, "Well, we have rather special clients here. We can't just have lawyers who want to sit in the back room and write briefs." We had never met before, and I could not fathom his reason for saying this. No second interview there.

> It was somewhat eye-opening to learn that my fellow Jews could be just as prejudiced as gentiles. That sort of diversity really makes you proud to be an American.

> I wonder what UConn's reaction would have been if a black applicant said that a white partner had told him, "Well, we can't just have lawyers who sit at their desks all day eating fried chicken and watermelon and saying 'Yo mutha' to the clients."

> Or if a female applicant said that a male partner had told her, "Well, we can't just have lawyers gossiping at their desks all day, doing their nails, and wanting time off during that special time of the month."

> Or if a physically challenged applicant said that a partner had told him, "This is a fast-paced action-oriented law firm, and we can't just have cripples wheeling around." Or if a homosexual reported that a partner had said, a la Philadelphia, "Well, we can't have AIDS in our men's room."

3. I had an interview with a family friend, the late Atty. Milton Sorokin. Milton was a member of the ACLU and a supporter of all causes liberal. UConn Law actually held a "Milton Sorokin Symposium" to celebrate his First Amendment work.

Milton listened to me politely, then said, "We have had older lawyers beginning here before, and there were always problems. They always wanted to start at the top." Needless to say, no job there.

Milton is deceased and unable to defend himself. No matter; he would deny it, while I would maintain that it happened exactly this way. I am willing to take a polygraph if anyone wants it.

Needless to say, if Milton had offered a stereotype of blacks or women or homosexuals or Muslims, there would have been hell to pay.

4. Late in the process, I had an interview with a very down-to-earth no-nonsense partner. It went very well. At the end he said to me, "Tell me, Michael, with a resumé like yours, why do you not yet have a job?"

Trying to be diplomatic, I said there could be 3 reasons: my record, my appearance, and my age. He replied that my record was excellent and my appearance fine. Nothing about age. It was the loudest silence that I have ever heard.

No job offer there either.

Other job interviews were more polite, but no jobs either; not even from the Connecticut Attorney General's Office.

It was now November 1987. Graduation was in May 1988, and still no job offers. I was getting really nervous.

George Schatzki was the Dean of UConn Law, and he and I got along well and spoke often. I wrote a letter to him explaining my situation and mentioned the possibility of age discrimination.

Two days later, during the evening class break at the coffee truck, Schatzki rushed up to me. He said that he had gotten my letter and was steamed. He said that he would personally investigate and would put a stop to the practice. At last, I thought, the good will prevail.

As I write, it is almost 40 years later, and I am still waiting for my answer.

Schatzki shafted me. Eventually he stopped communicating with me altogether. My assumption is that he made a few phone calls and was politely told where to get off. He later became Dean at another law school; so much for promoting the successful.

Dean Schatzki did one thing, however.

He facilitated a meeting between me and Atty. Nancy Dart, who was then head of the UConn Placement Office (now called Career Development). When we met, I first discussed the R&C interview mentioned above. Nancy said that she was already aware of that, and had contacted the interviewer, a friend of hers. His version of events was totally different from mine. He was not enthusiastic and had never virtually promised me a job with a senior partner. Nancy smirked at me in disbelief.

Thus, Nancy politely called me a liar and would not investigate further.

Eventually, I landed a job with a slavedriver which did not last long, and then hung out a shingle and went into business for myself. However, like the Armenians who never gave up trying to get justice, I continued to write.

I contacted future UConn Law Deans, including Hugh Macgill, Nell Jessup Newton, Jeremy Paul, Timothy Fisher, and Eboni S. Nelson. No help.

To be fair, the late Dean Macgill did one thing.

UConn Law had the habit of assigning alumni to call other alumni to ask for donations. For some reason, I always got a female caller. I would ask her if she herself would donate to a law school which permitting firms that discriminated against females to recruit on campus. When the caller said No, I explained what had happened to me, and asked why I should donate to a school that countenanced age discrimination.

Apparently, these remarks got back to Dean Macgill, who caused my name to be removed from the list of alumni called for donations. I have not been called in years, or gotten letters asking for money.

I thus stand as the only person in American history, to my knowledge, to have been personally singled out and kicked off of a fund-raising mailing (and telephonic) list, although I had committed no crime and had incurred no community-wide odium. My offense was to speak my mind at a law school that trumpets its commitment to the First Amendment a la Milton Sorokin.

Dean Macgill was once Chairman of the Connecticut State Ethics Commission, an irony lost on no one.

I must say that the late Dean Macgill deserves an award as Law School Administrator of the Century, for his coup in purging me, Stalin-style, from the fund-raising rolls.

Dean Paul kindly took the trouble to remind me that the law school already had a policy prohibiting firms that recruit on campus from discriminating and sent me a copy of that policy.

In the 1950's, the Klan took out a full-page ad in the New York Times, explaining that it was for 100% Americanism, without regard to race, color or creed. That ad, while in writing, probably persuaded no one, any more than Dean Paul's written policy persuaded anyone. A total bureaucratic cop-out.

I was hopeful when Dean Timothy Fisher took over. After all, he was described as a no-nonsense, dynamic, charismatic man.

I sent him a copy of my prior write-up. He replied that it contained interesting points, but he would not take any action "at this time." I asked him when he would take action, and if he would conduct an investigation and invite me to testify. He replied that my letter "was not helpful." I heard nothing from him since.

I thought I would do better with the current Dean, Eboni S. Nelson. She is a black lady from South Carolina, and thus needs no lessons in discrimination. Still, she would not risk her career to say anything.

Of course, Deans are subservient to the school's central administration. Perhaps UConn itself would do better.

I wrote to the UConn Central Administration in Storrs, which did absolutely nothing. Except once.

UConn had an employee named Scott Brohinsky. He worked in something called "Government Relations", meaning that he was a lobbyist disguised as a legislative liaison. Those folks take taxpayer money for their salaries and expenses, and use it to lobby for yet more taxpayer funding. Quite a good deal.

Brohinsky wrote me a sarcastic letter stating that he had read my "constant complaints", and that UConn had investigated those complaints and found nothing.

Actually, there had been no investigation. I had never, and to this day have not, received any report of any investigation explaining the facts and investigation methodology and witnesses, with report conclusions and reasons therefor. I was never even called as a witness! The reason is obvious: UConn knows that it could not withstand a real investigation, and feels no media pressure to conduct one.

I asked Brohinsky that if he heard complaints that UConn participated in discrimination against lawyers of Polish ancestry, or black or women lawyers, he would sarcastically write of their "constant complaints." No answer, of course.

I also tried the UConn Board of Trustees. No help.

Atty. Lewis B. Rome wrote to me that the President of UConn should manage UConn. Fair enough, but what if he or she doesn't manage it well? I trust that Atty. Rome is more demanding in his own law practice.

Roger Gelfenbein, a longtime Hartford cheerleader, politely told me to get lost. This is the same man who had his house listed in his wife's name, ostensibly to avoid creditors as skillfully as he avoided me.

Finally, there is the "Board of Governors for Higher Education", which is supposed to have some control over UConn. Repeated letters to the Board went unanswered.

Non-residents of Connecticut may wonder how UConn gets away with this. The answer is that Connecticut, as a state, is a shell of its former self. One of the best states in the country when I was growing up in the 50's, Connecticut is now a high-tax, high-expense, government-employee haven whose residents want only to get out; or at least to drastically change the economy.

The political leadership's response is to gamble and smoke our way to prosperity; a pipe dream, no pun intended.

The only major source of pride for Connecticut residents is the UConn girls' and boys'

basketball teams; and occasionally the football team. Connecticut will do nothing to stifle these; and thus, UConn is sacrosanct. Trying to reform UConn is like trying to get the Pope to convert to Islam. UConn stands perpetually aloof in its arrogance regarding criticism, acting only when pressured by the media.

We had better hope that Geno Auriemma and Dan Hurley, the two highest-paid state employees, live forever.

I called four area lawyers who were good friends of mine. They all responded alike, as if I were listening to the same CD: of course there is age discrimination in law firm hiring. What did you think?

One of those lawyers was an old boyhood friend. A mild-mannered, quiet soul, he called me back and was positively apoplectic, to the point where I hardly recognized him. "Michael! What did you expect? Are you so stupid that you really believed that lawyers followed the law? What is the matter with you, Michael? I cannot believe your ignorance. And don't bother to fight it. Even if you win, you will lose. No one will ever talk to you again, and you'll get nowhere. Stay on your own!"

I also spoke to several of my classmates who were older. One, a bright woman with a Ph.D., in her early forties, said that she had long ago given up on even hoping for a downtown law job.

There was one bright note. Dr. Maryann Michaels was the former Dean of Admissions at UConn Law. Years ago, she had helped me out when I applied to the school. Dr. Michaels had the decency to tell me that this sort of thing had been going on for decades, and that UConn Law was well aware of it. Of course, she is no longer at the school.

People may indeed wonder why there is a problem. After all, UConn always trumpets its commitment to DEI. Why not equity for older students?

The reason is surprisingly simple: UConn does not want to offend the big firms, on which it depends for getting its graduates employed, and feels no media pressure to do so.

It is all a political game.

Since this could be considered a political matter, I went to the politicians.

My State Senator, Tony Guglielmo, a friend, refused to help. Too many UConn alumni in his district. He would not even investigate the matter.

My State Representative, Chris Davis, was a UConn grad student. No help there either.

Federal legislators responded only with form letters from staff.

I had been a member of the Connecticut Bar Association (CBA) for years and assumed it would help. But the CBA would not touch the matter. Its journal, The Connecticut Lawyer, consistently rejected my articles publicizing illegal age discrimination in law firm hiring. A former editor, Lewis Parker, politely explained to me that while I "make some very interesting points, this topic does not provide the kind of nuts-and-bolts legal information that we try to provide to our readers."

If you read the journal today, you will find it saturated with articles and conferences on DEI. This is nuts and bolts? Of course, the CBA does not want to offend the big firms, any more than the UConn Law School wants to alienate them.

The CBA has a "Human Rights" section. The Chairman at the time, Atty. Barbara J. Collins of Hartford, explained to me that age discrimination might be important, but it would have to take a back seat to such matters as revoking the death penalty for the horrific Petit murderers, and countering alleged discrimination by the bar examining committee against law graduates with psychological and substance abuse problems. I am still waiting to hear more from the section.

Another fellow, Atty. Burt Cohen, was Chairman of the CBA's Diversity Committee. I sent him information, and asked what he would do about illegal age discrimination. He patiently explained that that issue "falls outside of the purview of the CBA Diversity Committee."

That is a reasonable strategy. If you want to get rid of an issue, simply define it away. Burt further suggested that I take up my concerns with the UConn Law School, citing the "new leadership" there.

There is no need for parody anymore. Truth is its own parody. But it's hard to be angry at someone who just wants to keep his job.

One CBA President was Atty. Karen DeMeola. She was also the Assistant Dean for Diversity at UConn Law [smile]. Karen ignored over a dozen of my letters asking that the CBA and UConn Law act on this problem. When I quit the CBA, she still ignored me, but did have a flunkie call me and ask, "how could we have enhanced your CBA experience?" Experience indeed. To repeat, you can't make this stuff up. The Hon. Karen DeMeola is now a Superior Court Judge. She is recognized by the CBA as a champion of diversity and equal rights.

The American Bar Association (ABA), as you might imagine, would not publish the matter. It is too busy pushing diversity and abortion.

I wrote to the ACLU but heard nothing. Apparently "civil liberties" extends to banning public school graduations from available churches that graciously volunteer their space, and getting physically- and sexually mature males to play in girls' sports, but not to fair employment for honorably discharged veterans.

Yes, I know: age discrimination is not sexy. But we pay taxes too.

But, in a pinch, there is always the media. Media pressure on wrongdoing can be devastating. Consider Watergate and numerous scandals since then.

The most liberal newspapers, including the New York Times and Washington Post, would not touch the story. TV exposé shows such as 60 Minutes, 20/20, and others were unresponsive. Of course, not enough public interest, as long as liberals are the ones doing the discrimination.

But even Fox News would not touch the story. I suggested a feature on "When Liberals Discriminate," but got nowhere. Again, not sexy enough.

When people ask me to give money to fight the discrimination du jour, I tell them that I will give as much, this year, as they gave to fight age discrimination last year. That usually gets curious looks. I suppose I could just mail them a copy of this essay.

Then some good news. On September 28, 2006, I received an e-mail from a lawyer in New York City. She had been appointed to a special committee of the New York State Bar Association (NYSBA) that was chartered to investigate illegal age discrimination in the legal profession. She searched the web, found my name, and invited me to give testimony.

The date was set for November 8, 2006. NYSBA was arranging a room in a New York City courthouse. Naturally, I would pay my own travel and incidental expenses, but it would be worth it. If New York, whose motto "Excelsior" means "Upward!" could publish on the subject, perhaps Connecticut would be next.

Then she wrote that the hearing would be postponed, but she would get back to me.

On November 8, 2006, which was, ironically, the original hearing date, came an e-mail with The Word: "The NYSBA Special Committee decided in a later October meeting not to hold any hearings at all."

Who got to New York? Could you imagine NYSBA cancelling hearings on race or gender discrimination?

I suggested that the Education Committee of the Connecticut General Assembly hold hearings on the subject of age discrimination in law firm hiring, as condoned by the taxpayer-supported University of Connecticut.

Committee staff should take measures to encourage the testimony of lawyers and former lawyers who are personally aware of the situation. Many will be reluctant to come forward. But they should be actively encouraged; just as people had to be encouraged to testify against race and gender discriminations in prior days.

Committee staff should ensure that UConn does not stonewall or evade or mislead the Committee. This will require full-time investigators, since UConn has substantial legal resources who naturally hope to advance their careers by any means necessary. Also, UConn has powerful friends who will spare no effort to protect the school even when it is in the wrong.

In other words, committee staff should be prepared for a fight no less grinding than the fight put up by Southern Senators during the passage of the Civil Rights Act. UConn means business.

Assuming that the hearings are positive, one possible legislative outcome appears as a proposed statute, below. The statute specifies, among other things, that prospective law students must be warned of the problem of illegal age discrimination in law firm hiring in advance. Reminds you of warning consumers about calorie counts in the food they plan to buy.

I realize this will never happen. . But it could help prospective older students. And who knows: it might even help school administrators to feel like human beings.

~~~

PROPOSED LEGISLATION: ONE POSSIBILITY
[NEW] C.G.S. Sec. 10a-xx.

(a) It is hereby found and determined that there is reasonable cause to believe that illegal age discrimination in law firm hiring exists in Connecticut, and that the University of Connecticut has been aware of the problem for decades, but is unwilling or unable to rectify the situation.

(b) It is hereby found and determined that it is in the best interest of this state to ensure that all persons applying to the University of Connecticut School of Law be made aware of this problem, and to discourage law firms from engaging in such practice. It is a matter of legislative determination that individuals and law firms in this state would benefit from the absence of age-related employment discriminatory practices.

(c) The Board of Governors of Higher Education shall, in consultation with the President of the University of Connecticut, ensure that the following policies are fully implemented and functioning by [reasonable date to be determined].

(1) That a letter is sent to the managing partner or similar person at all law firms which use the facilities of the UConn Law School for recruitment purposes, making it clear that illegal age discrimination in law firm hiring will not be tolerated. Such letter is to be limited to the issue of age discrimination only, notwithstanding that letters regarding other discriminations might also be sent. Such letter is to be signed by

the President of UConn and the Dean of the UConn Law School, and will be sent no later than August 1 of each year.

(2) That all UConn Law School materials, whether in print or online, which might reasonably be read by prospective students, contain a clear and conspicuous warning that the problem of illegal age discrimination in law firm hiring is known to exist, that UConn is taking active measures to combat the problem, but that students must be aware that success cannot be guaranteed.

(3) That UConn Law create, fund, establish and maintain an office to receive complaints of age discrimination in hiring, which actively investigates such complaints, prepares written reports in response to each complaint, and has the power to bar offending law firms from recruiting on campus and publish the names of firms so barred.

(d) The Board of Governors of Higher Education shall report annually to the General Assembly on the activities undertaken in accordance with subsection (c) of this section. The report shall include actual implementation efforts, plans, examples of implementation paperwork, and such statistics as are necessary to ensure that the goals of this section are being achieved.

(e) If the General Assembly determines that the goals of this section are not being satisfactorily achieved, it has the power to order such actions as are necessary and proper to achieve those goals.

~~~

Twist and turn as it might, and employ every legal trick in the book, UConn cannot deny the fact of illegal age discrimination in law firm hiring and its willing complicity therein.

The result is that I am forced to pay taxes to support a State institution that actively participated in age discrimination against me.

As I write, virtually the entire Democrat Party is bending over backwards to support the "rights" of an illegal El Salvadorean criminal gang member who never should have been in this country in the first place. He snuck in here, and now is trying to use our legal system to his advantage. Yet not one Democrat goes to bat for the rights of a productive citizen, an honorably discharged veteran and patriot, who was illegally discriminated against. Not that the Republicans were any help. Not one Democrat goes to bat for the rights of innocent citizens killed and maimed by illegals. Great thing, this partisanship.

At least UConn Law School was a high-quality and affordable education. No complaints there.

But please, don't ever try to sell DEI to me.

ACKNOWLEDGEMENTS

Please bear with me, as I have several people to thank.

My second-grade teacher, the late Catherine M. Buteau. She defied the rules of the day and taught me multiplication, because she thought I could catch on. It taught me to think outside the box.

My seventh-grade English teacher, the late Evelyn Adams. She was a stickler for grammar. She once wrote on the blackboard: IT'S = IT IS. I never forgot it. Yet today, even some lawyers put in an apostrophe every time they see an "s" at the end of a word.

My high school history teachers, the late John Gale and the late Helen Rives. They lit the fires of knowledge with living history and respect for the justice system. Mr. Gale was disappointed that I did not become a teacher, although today he would have understood.

My Western Civilization professor, the late Dr. Peter B. Kenen, who taught the great texts of philosophy and turned me into a thinker.

My basic training sergeant, Wallace A. Smith. He said "Gentlemen, you will never forget me." And we didn't. He at least instilled the idea of discipline.

My English Literature professor, the late Dr. Frank Chiarenza, whose love of learning was unexcelled and his guidance unequalled. He was a master of the English language.

My law professors, particularly the late Cornelius Scanlon, the late Nathan Levy, and the late Alan Cullison. They were true gentlemen and scholars.

My late mother, who never got to see me finish law school. She would have wondered why this essay even had to be written.

My late wife Pat. I was frustrated with the insurance bureaucracy and wanted to go to law school, but afraid I was too old. "How old will you be if you don't go?" she asked. That did it.

My wife Harriet. A former paralegal, she patiently put up with the demands of lawyering. She always encouraged me to finish this book when the going got rough. I could not have done it without her.

My former law associate, Atty. Jessica L. Audet. She was the greatest of CPS defense lawyers. She won cases that seemed impossible.

My former litigation paralegal, Lisa Malone, without whose help I could not have won the court cases that I did. She was on top of everything.

My former office manager and paralegal, Karen Thibodeau. She started with me when I had only an old-fashioned word processor and very little money coming in. She stayed through thick and thin, and ended up as the glue that kept the office together.

Mark Sherman, Esq., who reviewed the manuscript. Mark is the founder of the Connecticut DCF Defenders Law Firm in Stamford, CT. It is currently the major law firm in the state concentrating in CPS defense. The firm includes seven lawyers, four of whom do CPS defense, plus a retired DCF investigative supervisor with 37 years' experience, and several paralegals.

The Director of Publishing at Defiance Press, Lisa Woodward, and her superb team of editors. It's one thing to know what you want to say. It's another to make it clear to the public. Lisa greatly helped this novice author say what had to be said.

Obviously, any errors in this essay are mine, and I take full responsibility.

www.ingramcontent.com/pod-product-compliance
Lightning Source LLC
Chambersburg PA
CBHW072048090426

42733CB00033B/2461